FOR BOB

*Calamity is the perfect glass wherein
we truly see and know ourselves.*

—WILLIAM DAVENANT

*Knowing others is intelligence;
knowing yourself is true wisdom.
Mastering others is strength;
mastering yourself is true power.*

—TAO TE CHING

ACKNOWLEDGMENTS

THIS BOOK WOULD not exist without the brave young people who expose their innermost thoughts and feelings every day in wilderness and other treatment settings. They set the bar high when it comes to being vulnerable, examining destructive patterns, taking accountability, and courageously reclaiming their lives. These young people have touched and inspired me.

This book would also not exist if it weren't for the parents of these young people who have called me up and asked for help! Parents can change and they have showed me time and again that small alterations in their parenting styles can create new, intimate, enduring, and emotionally close bonds with their adolescent and young adult children.

I was lucky enough to be mentored by some of the best wilderness therapists, whom I started learning from right out of college. Thank you to: Pam Parsons, LMFT, Brad Reedy, Ph.D., Cheryl Kehl, LCSW, Matt Hoag, Ph.D., and Devon Glissmeyer, Ph.D.

My business, Parallel Process, which led me on this path to more deeply understand the parent's experience, would not exist if it weren't for my trusted friend and colleague Scott Hall. Scott has believed in me as a clinician wholeheartedly and for that I am grateful, thank you!

This book has been churning in my consciousness for at least eight years, and there are many individuals who helped bring it to fruition:

I have dedicated this book to my husband, Bob Whittaker. It has always been a dream of mine to write a book and I am lucky enough to have a partner who deeply understands that that is what life is for: pursuing dreams. He not only supported me in the writing process, his eyes were the first to glance at my chapters and I am deeply grateful for his editorial critiques, praise, love, and most importantly, patience. Thank you.

I owe a special thanks to a good friend and colleague, Emily Miranda, LCSW. While on her own sabbatical from adolescent therapy, Emily was in a unique place to shed her clinical insight (via Skype) and editorial knowledge to my chapters. Thank you!! I would also like to thank Emily Faber, LCSW, Ben Mason, M.Ed., and Josh Doyle, M.Ed., for reading my manuscript and keeping me moving forward with writing and pursuing publication. I could not have written this book without the encouragement of colleagues from the treatment field.

My dear friend, Jessie Kaufman, LCSW, who is a clinician and a mother, said to me at the onset of the project, "Krissy, it is probably a pipe dream for you to write a mystery novel, but it is not a pipe dream to write a book for parents with kids in treatment." It cannot be overstated how much her nudge helped jump-start my project. Furthermore, her sharp instincts helped refine my thinking about how I present my book, for this I am grateful. Thank you.

I want to thank my mother, Ellie Pozatek-Hardy, also a clinician, for her strong endorsement of the book and its content. I want to thank my father, Zig Pozatek, for the thought and care he put into my education—thank you.

I feel grateful to have found Lantern Books. I want to thank Gene Gollogly for his kindness and his enthusiasm for my book. I also want to thank Kara Davis for guiding me through the process and for the sharp editorial skills of Martin Rowe.

Lastly, I want to thank Dave Wolman, Alan Boye, Hillery Hinds Maxymillian, and my close friends and family who have been supportive though the journey, thank you!

CONTENTS

AUTHOR'S NOTE

ALL OF THE stories used in the following chapters mirror real parent–child relationship problems stemming from my clinical experience as both an adolescent and parent therapist. Yet each case study is a composite that integrate congruent themes from a variety of cases into fictional vignettes. In adolescent treatment programs, common parent–child patterns are frequently observed. However, none of the vignettes resemble any one client and/or family.

Though my professional experience comes from within wilderness-therapy programs, the concepts outlined in this book apply to any parent who has a child in treatment for mental health and/or behavioral issues. Whether your child is in an outpatient treatment program while living at home or is placed in an inpatient, residential, or wilderness-treatment program, the Parallel Process, the process for parents, remains the same.

This book focuses on the parents' process; it is not a recommendation for any type of specific treatment for your child. This book is also not intended to be used as an alternative to seeking the professional help of a therapist or other support system.

Please note that in order to be inclusive, I've alternated back and forth between his, her, son, daughter, mom, and dad. The parent–child dynamics discussed in this book are not exclusively those of mothers or fathers, sons or daughters. I've used a variety of pronouns because, in my experience, these dynamics exist in every combination.

PREFACE

PARENTING IS THE hardest job there is; no parent gets it completely right. Every parent has shortcomings. We're only human. What makes the content of this book so challenging is that parents can give a hundred percent, yet be slightly off-target, as no one can fully see their own patterns. To have a child engage in self-destructive behaviors can cause parents to feel inundated with shame, and lead to strong defenses. This book is about using the crisis of having a child in treatment as an opportunity to open up to those blind spots we all have in our parenting.

I write this book with a deep compassion for parents in this process. I worked with adolescents and parents for eight years before I became a parent myself. As a mother of two daughters, I know intimately the intense pressures that parents face. Whether it's getting enough sleep, paying the bills, figuring out daycare and schools, managing daily life, cooking meals, balancing work/home pressures, and finding time for one's marriage, the challenges are never-ending. In addition to all these daily stressors, having a child who's struggling is enormously painful.

Yet in over a decade of working with such adolescents, I've found that many parents remain stuck in negative dynamics and parenting styles that aren't working. Moreover, these discordant parent–child patterns are not getting the therapeutic attention they need and deserve.

My hope is that as parents you can identify with some of the patterns I illustrate and in the process grasp a deeper awareness of where you may be unintentionally reinforcing negative behaviors or undermining your child's emotional development. With this awareness, you can better support your child's development toward positive independence.

What I call the Parallel Process is when parents engage therapeutically alongside their child, to understand their own thoughts, feelings, and behaviors. Not only do parents need to support their kids as they make the painful and turbulent transition from adolescence to adulthood, but more importantly they need to learn to relate to their child differently during treatment and beyond. Parents can only do this through enhancing their own self-knowledge. The intent of this book is not to blame parents for their child's problems, but to highlight negative patterns that many fall into and to empower parents to begin a new relationship with their child.

part 1

THE PARENT–CHILD PROBLEM

THE JOURNEY OF A WILDERNESS THERAPIST

THE MID-DAY SUN hung in the sky above a ridge in the high Utah desert, casting a golden glow on the juniper trees and sagebrush visible on an opposing ridge roughly a hundred yards away. From behind the trees, twenty blindfolded parents slowly came into sight, gently guided up to the ridge by the wilderness instructors facilitating the parents' experience. On the other ridge, I stood with twelve dirty and enthusiastic adolescents who'd just completed roughly fifty days in the desert away from their parents in an attempt to decipher the emotional and behavioral problems that had overtaken them. They, too, were blindfolded.

We received a signal that it was time to guide the teens to the edge of the ridge to prepare them to see their parents. We found our spots and held a brief moment of silence as everyone paused, took a deep breath, and collected their thoughts, intentions, and prayers. It was as though each student was on the edge of his or her own emotional precipice, preparing to leap into the unknown. At a precise moment, parents and teens were instructed to take off their blindfolds and proceed down the valley toward each other, literally and figuratively bridging the gulf between them.

Although I'd observed this type of family reunion many times before, I found it impossible not to be moved. Some of the teenagers bolted openheartedly toward their parents with a mixture of fearlessness and vulnerability. Others were more reluctant and shy, but equally steadfast in their determination to keep going. With each step, fortitude trumped trepidation. In spite of what had existed before the journey into the wilderness, the love between parent and child was evident. Most reunions were accompanied by hugs, tears, and relief; some still contained a painful distance. Yet the space of two months had enabled the parents and kids alike to look inward in an attempt to see each other with fresh eyes.

Knowing the hardships these children faced during their wilderness experience, I found it heartening to see these once troubled adolescents earnestly engage their parents. They felt proud, and they wanted their parents to notice they were different. These adolescents still faced a daunting road ahead. But for a brief time, they could celebrate what they had accomplished—a reunion with their parents, with a changed perspective and some new skills, and a few life lessons under their belt.

―――――――――

FOURTEEN YEARS AGO, I was dropped off in the middle of nowhere Utah to begin my training as a field instructor for a wilderness-therapy program. I was eager to learn how to build rapport with these closed-off, self-absorbed, and defiant teens. I underwent my own "boot camp," working first with boys and girls who'd been through the courts and then at-risk adolescents. Through my own trial and error, I discerned the essential ingredients that enable an individual to break through to a shut-down, troubled teen. These include: demonstrating authority through clear boundaries; attuning emotionally; validating and reflectively listening to the teen; reframing issues and problems; and most importantly, letting the kids struggle within the structure, or container, of the program. I studied seasoned instructors, I scrutinized therapy sessions, and I devoured every book relating to the daunting period of life that is adolescence. With the right combination of these key critical ingredients—a little of this, a dash of that, and a gentle stir—kids responded. I found it at once enlightening and empowering to feel effective. It was an honor to know these young people and, in the process, I discovered how much I genuinely liked them.

Little did I know that this experience would set in motion changes to my own life and its direction. I was humbled at the profound impact wilderness therapy has on struggling, broken, and immature teens. I saw life and energy reawaken the hidden, inner world of these young people, as if a light had been turned on. The glow illuminated and exposed their thoughts and feelings. The teenagers began to use "feeling" words instead of behaviors to communicate. Cognition replaced emotionality. They'd grasped something intangible during their journey, and had begun the process of reclaiming their life.

As these kids pulled themselves out of their protective shells in an effort to come to know their authentic selves, I wondered: "What is it about wilderness that causes this transformation?" Was it the fresh air or the altered state of being in a new landscape? Was it the stripping away of everything familiar and removal of the trappings of modern life? Was it the exercise; the good, healthy fun; or the balanced diet? Was it the skilled therapists and wilderness instructors? Of course, all of these factors contributed. Still, after nearly a decade as a wilderness therapist, it became evident to me that one, further critical factor contributed: the struggling teen was extracted from home, and the troubled parent–child dynamic was temporarily disrupted.

When adolescent behavior in the home escalates to extremes, parents may feel emotionally at the end of their rope. Their children are manipulative and angry, either having tantrums and yelling at them or silent and isolating themselves in their bedrooms. Parents attempt to get through each day, tiptoeing around landmines. Nothing to stop this situation seems effective anymore: these adolescents ignore the consequences of their actions, regularly traduce boundaries, don't respond to incentives, and shrug off the threats. Troubled teens are beyond rationality and logical reasoning and parents don't know how to respond to each new episode of poor behavior. If the teenager's behavior is more serious—including substance abuse, sexual promiscuity, self-harming, running away, a refusal to go to school, and self-isolation within the home—parents are desperate to steer their child back to safety. A treatment program provides a temporary sigh of relief until the next chapter of angst begins.

In the wilderness program, the first contact teenagers make with their parents is through pen and paper. Predictably, the initial letters parents receive are full of statements such as "I will hate you forever" or "I promise if you bring me home, I will do whatever you ask!" In essence, these letters express the child's grasp for the old status quo in his relationship with his parents. The underlying messages are: "I want to stay connected to you, even if it's just fighting and conflict, because it's familiar," or "I don't really want to be responsible for myself; I'd rather keep negotiating with you." Because mom and dad have been subtracted from the child's day-to-day life, the child misses the object (parents) to push and pull against. Without her parents, the child is left to confront her own internal struggles and conflicts.

Removing the cushion of parents is a startling loss for children, and they begin to go through the stages of grief for the death of their "old lives." They deny that they need help, become angry they were being sent away, start to bargain with their parents to bring them home, and fall into depression because they can't change their situation. Eventually, they learn acceptance.[1] Parents send teens and young adults into treatment because they're desperate for them to examine their self-harming choices and hope they'll trade in these negative habits for healthy ones. Yet what also comes with separating parent and child is that kids are left in charge of their own problem-solving.

The initial weeks of wilderness therapy are fraught with struggle, defiance, and resistance, which eventually give way to acceptance.

When resistant teens arrive at this place of acceptance, they become present. They're not rehashing the past or plotting their escape, but are settling into a new state. The intervention has captured their full attention. Attuned clinicians and instructors start to see an adolescent who's curious, open, and exhibits a degree of autonomy. Being away from the familiar environment of home has brought with it the freedom and opportunity to start over with a fresh slate. Most importantly, the space that was once filled with emotional turbulence has been opened and a new cognitive clarity has taken its place. The kids now have energy available for them to learn.

When their chronic attempts to manipulate their external environment (by using excuses, finding loopholes, acting helpless, and so on) no longer work, teens are left with only one choice: to adapt their internal environment. They begin to engage impressively in their own emotional work. They learn to identify their past "poor" choices and how to express their feelings. They talk openly in groups, with ease. They learn to give and accept feedback. They take on positive role-modeling. They show emotional vulnerability; they become accountable; they identify their patterns. They actually start to write their parents because they *want* to share. They become leaders. Last but not least, they start to feel in charge of themselves again, and begin to approach situations through a cognitive process, rather than merely react to them. It is as if they have stepped off the emotional roller coaster which was once driving their life. They see that in every new moment they have choices.

Parents, on the other hand, are watching anxiously on the sidelines, still in their patterns. They may feel relief initially that their child is safe, but swiftly they resume their anxiety and worry. They're overeating and not sleeping; they're chronically tense, drinking too much, or feeling depressed and withdrawn. Some feel a pervasive unrest. Some may be in therapy, but the content of each session is filled-up with their child. Parents struggle with deep feelings of regret and failure; many have admitted that when they're not distracted by work, they think of their child incessantly. They miss him, feel guilty for sending him away, resentful or angry about the past, and anxious about everything else. To compound the distress, parents are at a loss as to what to tell their family, friends, and community. In short, parents aren't in an emotionally healthy place: they're bogged down and trapped, as though they cannot feel anything different until their child changes.

In the family reunion at the end of the program, as described above, the contrast between parents and children is evident. Kids look into their parents' eyes, show vulnerability, take accountability for their past behaviors, and express calmness—a feeling of being "at ease." Though thrilled to see these changes, parents still toil with their own self-awareness. They're guarded and uncertain at how to proceed and relate differently to their child. They stumble awkwardly and embarrassedly through "I feel" statements. These hard-earned changes in the child become tenuous when only one side of the relationship equation has changed. For long-term success, the *whole family* has to operate differently. If kids are sent out of the home, stripped of everything familiar, asked to be vulnerable, look at their patterns, learn new skills, and address their problematic behaviors, shouldn't parents be willing to do this as well?

How a family operates isn't the primary focus of treatment programs, because the child is the identified client. Parents are seen predominantly as functional and responsible adults—after all, the child is the one who's lying, skipping school, harming herself, delaying his education, and potentially ruining her future. She's the one sent to treatment. However, from a family-system's perspective,[2] the home won't change unless the parents *also* examine their contributions to the discordant parent–child dynamics. Many parents have been so entangled in their child's struggles for years, they've assumed certain roles: rescuer, lecturer, fixer, enabler, or yeller. Others have shut down emotionally and withdrawn, avoiding the home, averting conflict, and incessantly looking for distractions.

It's my belief that parents can embark on their own journey of self-discovery and acquire the same skills their adolescent has excelled at learning: to become aware of their own feelings, to use "I feel" statements and assertive communication, to take accountability for behavior they regret. Like their children, they can use reflective listening, identify negative patterns, model sharing and open dialogue (the way parents want their child to talk to them), learn the art of reframing, attune to their child, and discover how to validate feelings. I will discuss all these skills in future chapters. Parents need to address these issues and develop these skills if the whole family is to operate in a healthy and a mutually satisfying way. I know first-hand that kids feel like "f—— ups."

But when parents admit that they're working on themselves as well, a little fresh air is brought into that parent–child relationship. When parents engage in their own self-reflection, a child feels relief at not being quite so under-the-microscope. Engaging in this "parallel process" enables parents to feel more in control through identifying their own patterns that are undermining the goal of their child developing into an independent, autonomous, accountable, and resilient individual.

From the outset, it should be understood that parents cannot *make* their child change; they can't make it all better. Hopefully, they *can* intervene to get their child into treatment. What they *can* do, in the meantime, is to become more self-aware and shift their responses and relate differently to their teens. Parents can un-trap themselves, and find their own inner calm and peace of mind—despite the behaviors their child chooses. They can develop skills to feel more at ease, while allowing and supporting their child to embark on their journey to recovery.

———

THIS IS THE theme of my program, the Parallel Process, and of this book. When I started working with parents, several said to me, "I need my own wilderness program." Many programs have wonderful workshops for parents, yet the emphasis is still on the child and his relationship with them. Parents worried they weren't changing enough—that they still felt anger, mistrust, and worry that interfered with seeing their child's progress. Parents needed their own tools.

At the outset of the Parallel Process, I was struck by how difficult it was to focus on parents' patterns and contributions. Parents are so entrenched in focusing on their child. During sessions, parents would raise concerns about, say, his education, her car at home, his cell phone, her friends calling. Then parents would shift to the treatment program: Would it meet their child's needs? What if their daughter wasn't being challenged enough, or manipulating the staff, or falling through the cracks? Was she failing to do the emotional work she needed to do? Then the dialogue would switch to planning the future: Where would he go next? How would they piece together his credits so he could graduate from high school or college? Finally, parents would ruminate and rehash the past, wondering why they their child chose drugs, or threw away her potential—why she ended up *here.*

Toward the end of every session, I would gently draw attention to the parents' process. I would attempt to expose the pattern each parent was engaging in: rescuing, fixing, ruminating, planning, solving, worrying, and despairing. At heart, what was missing was *self-awareness*—ironically, the very same thing their children were learning in treatment. Before they'd learned self-awareness on the program, these teenagers had acted out without going through a cognitive process, and rarely considered consequences. With self-awareness, kids and adults have choices.

Now it was the parents' turn to apply these lessons: to stay with uncomfortable feelings, break their patterns, and develop self-awareness. The Parallel Process switches the focus to the parents, and encourages their own self-discovery.

My hope for this book is that when you, as a parent, feel distraught, reactive, and despairing, you can use the tools outlined herein to reflect on your own internal process. By becoming aware of your thoughts and feelings, you can *choose* how you want to proceed. You can feel powerful again, and model emotional health for your kids and communicate assertively with them. You can set boundaries and hold your teen accountable; reframe problems and empower your young adult to solve them. You can learn validation and emotional attunement, and break your own patterns. You can find contentment again. *These may be the only things you have control over.*

chapter 1

THE ENTANGLED PARENT

THE FUNDAMENTAL TRAIT that exists in every young person who's sent to a wilderness or therapeutic program is what I call **inadequate internal resources** to manage the stresses and strains of growing up in this society. Parents don't cause this trait directly, since a myriad of influences shape children, as evidenced by the fact that many of these families have other children thriving at home. Yet parenting approaches can inadvertently reinforce this pattern of poor resiliency and dependence.

Many of the kids who enter treatment have had sensitivities and vulnerabilities as children. Sensing these fragilities, parents work to help, protect, and advocate for their child. The child may have attention-deficit disorders or learning issues. She may be impulsive or become excessively angry and throw tantrums. He may be socially anxious and find it difficult to separate from his parents and make friends. The family may have gone through depression, divorce, or another conflict. There may have been some form of childhood trauma, an adoption, or a death in the family. Whatever they may be, these are some of the many issues that kids face in childhood and pre-adolescence that can lead to more serious behavioral and emotional problems in adolescence. In response to these vulnerabilities, many parents become more involved in monitoring their child, praising and rescuing him from hardships. In short, parents become *over-involved*.

What begins as a nurturing response, can escalate into entrenched parent–child patterns that can be hard for either the parent or child to shake. You may have heard the terms: "helicopter parents," "rescuers," "enmeshment," "codependency." These parents are making good-faith attempts to help their son or daughter. However, most aren't aware of their own anxiety, which is driving their over-involvement, or the underlying messages that over-involvement sends ("you can't do it yourself"). They can't see the disabling and disruptive pattern that over-involvement sets up.

All parents want to soothe and comfort their children. This primal instinct is hard-wired into the neurobiology of mammals. It enables the parent to feel bonded to the child and vice versa, which creates a secure base for small children and is essential developmentally.[3] It's also one of the true joys of parenting: to have a child run to you for a hug when she's frightened or hurt. It *matters* when you can soothe your child in a way that no one else can.

Yet, when babies and toddlers grow up, they need to develop their own self-soothing skills. The transition is challenging, and at times both parents and children resist it. Parents feel the urge to solve problems and children become accustomed to and dependent on it. The ability for a parent to "fix" something can be an expression of love, and in return, the child feels loved.

When a child is struggling emotionally or has some special needs, it's even harder for a parent to refrain and let the child try to solve her own problem. Parents often overcompensate for any deficiencies their child might have, and over-involvement can lead to enmeshment and codependency. With this dynamic, it's extremely hard for adolescents to develop the internal resources necessary for confidence and resiliency in adult life: the ability to solve problems, to set goals, to work hard, to delay gratification, to motivate yourself, to regulate your emotions, be disciplined, and to uncover your talents and potential.

MATT AND PEGGY

Matt was Peggy and Mark's second child. Their first, Sarah, was always self-sufficient, adaptable, and easy-going. Matt found it harder to separate from his mother at a young age and seemed more dependent on her. He was socially awkward, struggled with reading others' social cues, and often had trouble with friends. Early on, he was diagnosed as having ADHD and dyslexia. He also had inconsolable tantrums through elementary school and beyond. Innately, Peggy could see her son's struggles and always provided extra help with his daily tasks—from cleaning his room, to getting him ready for school on time, to completing his homework.

As her son grew, Matt and Peggy's pattern became more established. They both felt they had a special bond whereby Matt needed his mom and she was compelled to help and assist him, while also advocating for him socially and educationally. Peggy never set boundaries or rules because she worried about Matt struggling and having low self-esteem. This seems like a natural, maternal response for a mother of a child with some special needs.

Yet problems began bubbling up with the onset of adolescence. Eighth grade was a tough year and by the ninth, things were going downhill fast. Although Matt was extremely dependent on his mother emotionally and otherwise, he began to resent her. The new social pressures of being a teenager impressed upon him that he didn't "need" Peggy. He began to ignore her, refuse her love or affection, and was rude and defiant. Because Matt and Peggy were so close, Matt knew how to hurt her and "push her buttons." He liked fighting in a way: he felt powerful when he could hurt her and get her to react. Matt was unhappy, so he wanted her to be unhappy as well.

To a degree, Matt also felt handicapped socially. A component of ADHD is feeling over-stimulated not only in the classroom but also in social contexts.[4] He was always missing the subtle social cues from peers. He perpetually felt left out, teased, or ignored. He never knew how to say the right thing, which further weighed on his tenuous self-esteem. With the escalation of all his struggles in adolescence, Matt was diagnosed with a mild form of depression, dysthymia.

Matt lacked internal motivation and as a result always quit sports teams a few weeks into the season. He became drawn to underachievers, which was a shortcut to drug use. Without any outlets for achievement and self-esteem, he began to smoke pot and lie about it to cope with his emotional pain. Pot was an instant solution to his emotional immaturity. He suddenly felt older, important, more mature, and more accepted, even cool. He didn't feel depressed and he laughed again. He solved his friend crisis, because now they all had a common interest: getting high. Most significantly, he felt independent of his mother.

Adolescence is demarcated developmentally as a time to individuate, to develop a sense of self, separate from your family of origin—also known as the differentiation of self.[5] It's a time when young people explore and hone their own thoughts, beliefs, and opinions to uncover what they want to move toward. Through testing their beliefs in the larger world, young people receive feedback about what they like and dislike, and what works and what doesn't. For emotionally immature adolescents, drugs actually feel like a way to grow up, to individuate. Yet, conversely, these teens are numbing themselves and further stunting their emotional, social, and cognitive development. Rather than maturing their internal environment, teens become dependent on something external: substances.

For Peggy, the situation was maddening. She knew adolescence was a hard phase for kids and parents alike, but she observed severe behavioral changes in Matt that she felt weren't normal. Matt would rage at her, at times becoming verbally abusive, even violent. Yet he still needed her to manage his life. He would fluctuate from wanting her close and pushing her away. As his demands, manipulations, and sense of entitlement escalated, Peggy tried to set limits; yet there was no track record of boundaries having been established. Moreover, when Matt was in this wild state, limits were impossible to enforce.

He was like a tornado that could blow in at any moment and destroy everything along its path. Peggy felt she'd lost her internal compass as to how to relate to Matt, as if she didn't even know him anymore. It felt chaotic. Peggy knew Matt had problems, but didn't know how to fix them. Should she back off? Should she put more energy into him? How should she deal with his angry behavior? In spite of everything, Matt desperately needed her to manage him, because he didn't know how to manage himself.

Meanwhile, there was more evidence of her son's destructive behavior: he smelled of marijuana; he was failing two subjects and not going to his tutor; he began to use the house like a hotel, expecting everything to be done for him; and his only interactions in the home were to ask for things. He rarely talked to his father and sister and often went straight to his room when he came home.

Peggy and her husband sought the help of an educational consultant to find a therapeutic program for Matt—an out-of-home placement. She never imagined that her life would have come to this, yet at this point Matt had to address multi-layered problems: drug use, depression, defiant behavior, anger, low self-esteem, failure at school, ADHD, dyslexia, and, last but not least, his relationship pattern with his parents.

Matt was placed in a wilderness-therapy program, which presented an opportunity for his parents to discover where and how they went off-track and discover what they could do differently, by engaging in a parallel process.

ENMESHED PARENTING

As a therapist for adolescents and parents, I frequently observe a problem in relationships that I've labeled as a "merged boundary" or **enmeshment**. The child engages in defiant, and at times reckless, behavior, but doesn't seem to fear any consequences or have any worries. The parent is doing all the worrying. Underneath this behavioral pattern, the child has a sense of self that is undifferentiated from the parent, meaning his sense of self is merged with his father or mother. The child doesn't feel wholly responsible for herself; she feels that every obstacle along the path is faced with mom or dad. When she gets an F in school, is expelled, or uses drugs, she thinks, "Mom will fix it, so I don't really have to change my behavior." Moreover, "If Mom doesn't fix it, I have a right to get mad at her, and blame her, because it's her responsibility." There's no remorse. The child never really feels affected by a failure. It affects his self-esteem, but the adolescent doesn't feel like his future, his education, or even his life is being harmed—because they don't feel their life is their *own*.

Enmeshed can be defined as being entangled.[6] Parents' emotions have become so entangled with their child's behavior that it's impossible to sort out what the parent is feeling internally and what emotional reaction the parent is having to the child's behavior. For example, a father might feel sad or anxious when he sees a son struggle with school, so his response is to come to the rescue. Or a mother might feel powerless at her daughter's inability to make friends, so her response is to lecture her. With this lack of awareness, it's also hard for parents to assess, and attune to, what their child is feeling underneath (inadequate, embarrassed, or hurt). Although enmeshed parents feel emotionally close to their children, Anne Katherine, author of *Boundaries: Where You End and I Begin*, writes: "Enmeshment, remember, may feel close, but it isn't. Enmeshment means someone's individuality is being squashed. An enmeshed person is not known."[7]

When a child feels that a parent shares responsibility for a failure, or for some kids is solely responsible, he doesn't feel the consequence of the failure and thus has no impetus for change. Likewise, the child may never feel the real reward of success. He may think, "I got an A on the paper to make my parents happy." The sense of achievement is absent because the boundary with the parent is merged, so it's hard to be differentiated: "Did I want this A, or did my dad want it?" This dependency on another person greatly interferes with a child's emotional development, sense of self, and personal autonomy, because she never truly feels she's done anything on her own.

But why would a child want to become so dependent on, and undifferentiated, from his parent? Mainly because it feels safe, and there are no real-life consequences. The world is scary, unknown, and daunting, while bargaining with mom and dad is familiar and comfortable. Not surprisingly, kids feel powerful when they can negotiate power at home. Many teens put all their energy into gaining control there since they lack the skills to feel powerful and confident in the world. For the adolescent, however, the damaging consequence of not building her own life is depression and despair, which can spur more acting out.

The same question applies to parents: Why would a parent want to become so responsible for and undifferentiated from his child? Enmeshment with a child allows a parent to feel close, intimate, and self-important. Many parents see their child as an extension of themselves, which validates the need to guide and steer his every move. Parents might complain about a child's dependency, yet their unconscious behavior is to perpetually reinforce this enmeshed boundary. Enmeshed parents may have their own fears and anxiety of abandonment, which are then projected onto the child. They may feel that separating from, or not providing constant support for, their child is desertion. Yet the consequences are damaging for parents as well. They may not be feeling their own emotions and living their own lives. They may never feel assured that their child has the skills to navigate life, which further perpetuates the pattern of hovering and analyzing their child's every move, even as he or she enters young adulthood and beyond.

CODEPENDENT PARENTING

Codependent parenting is a more extreme version of enmeshed parenting. It happens when the child and parent's identity and emotions become so intertwined that both are assuming roles. The parent is not only emotionally managing her child, but the child is doing the same with her mom or dad. These dynamics often exist when there's an exclusive relationship between a single child and a single parent—whether because of divorce, the death of a parent, or with an emotionally distant marriage where one parent gets his or her emotional needs met exclusively through the child. In this case dependency, rescuing, and emotional manipulation become the norm. The child is dependent on the parent to fix problems with no boundaries or consequences; the parent is equally dependent on the child to meet his emotional need for closeness and intimacy because he has no close connection to a spouse or partner.

In codependent parenting, the child believes the parent's job is to make him happy, de-escalate anger, and soothe sadness, while the parent often loses sight of her own feelings. Melody Beattie, author of *Codependent No More*, writes that codependency is, "losing yourself in other people. Feeling emotions of others and not your own."[8] For example, when a daughter lies to her father and then gets caught and feels guilty, she still wants dad to help take the guilt away, to manage her emotions. Dad loses sight of his own feelings of anger or betrayal and goes to comfort his daughter, to make it better. The daughter's emotions become the central focus and the father's feelings are secondary or non-existent. This inevitably allows the daughter a great deal of power to control her father and make him feel guilty. Yet, dad endorses this arrangement, because he wants his daughter to talk to when he needs to vent his problems. Children in codependent relationships are much more exposed to the adult world and are often privy to financial matters, details of marriages and adult relationships, and other adult stressors. Yet these teens don't have the internal skills to handle them.

In parent–child codependency, the parent and child feel at a deep level that they are the most important person in each other's life. On one level, this relationship feels close, comfortable, even stable. However, it can easily become unstable and based on manipulation and control. For example, if the parent tries to date or even remarries, the child may act out and sabotage the relationship because he perceives it as a threat to his own one with the parent. The power dynamic in the family is skewed. There isn't a boundary where the parent is the authority figure; the child feels she has equal footing with the parent. This can lead to a dynamic where both manipulate the other into doing what they want the other to do.

Likewise, if the child begins to turn away from his parent and engage in risky behavior, such as drug use, it's hard for the parent to confront it because she fears her child may become more distant and secretive, which would disrupt their intimacy and closeness. As a result, the parent may move deeper into rescue mode by allowing a certain degree of poor behavior. I've seen parents overlook or endorse the use of pot in the house since the codependent parent is too fearful of conflict to enforce a boundary. As a result, the adolescent lacks a sense of personal consequence and personal responsibility, and loses the ability to undergo healthy individuation and maturation.

SASHA AND JANE

Sasha was sixteen years old, and on the surface the epitome of a healthy teen with a close relationship with her mother, Jane. She was avidly engaged in school and community activities: book club, drama club, honor roll, and softball. Her mother seemed to follow her every footstep: coaching the softball team, reading in the book group, and volunteering to chaperone school activities. Sasha even referred to her mother as her "best friend."

Jane and her husband had divorced when Sasha was three. Subsequently, Sasha's relationship with her father had faded, resulting in her strong attachment to her mother and Jane's to her. They felt it was the two of them against the world. When Sasha was eight, her mother remarried, and Sasha feared this would disrupt their close relationship. To cope with this fear, Sasha never accepted her stepfather and continued to have an exclusive relationship with her mother. It wasn't personal, yet she perceived her stepfather as the enemy who took her mother away. Not surprisingly, the stepfather was never really able to integrate into the family and always felt on the sidelines. He got his wife's attention only second to her daughter.

While it's normal to have readjustments to a family system with a remarriage, Jane felt deeply guilty for what she'd "done" to Sasha. She began to acquiesce to her daughter, and consequently Sasha became more demanding, entitled, and manipulative. Their relationship became an unspoken contract: "I'll let you marry stepdad, if you allow me more freedom and privileges." Jane became over-involved in her daughter's life because of her guilt—she wanted Sasha to still feel loved. Yet this seemed to only fuel Sasha's need for more control, because all the boundaries in the home became moveable, and her sense of security was disrupted. In her emotional upheaval, Sasha began experimenting with high-risk behavior, which eventually led to a methamphetamine (meth) addiction.

In therapy, Sasha reluctantly admitted to me that she liked meth because it was one thing that her mother couldn't control. It made her feel free, like she had a life that was only hers. Still, she asserted that it was a way to hurt her mother, not noticing how meth was harming her. Because she lacked parental boundaries to struggle within, and emotional space within which to individuate and develop her own thoughts and beliefs, Sasha assumed that the only way to have her own self was to rebel. She wanted to have secrets to create distance and space between her and her mother. Yet she also felt terribly guilty and sorry for hurting her mother. Her method of individuation, though deeply flawed, was to harm herself.

This dynamic is typical of parent–child codependency. The daughter is managing her mother's guilt for divorcing and remarrying, by acting as though they are best friends, and turning to her mother for comfort (while keeping secrets). The mother is emotionally managing her daughter by comforting her, ceding boundaries, and allowing her more privileges and freedoms (i.e.: to manipulate and control the home). Neither is accountable for her own behavior.

This arrangement is far too common in households where a child is overly attached to one parent, and a quid-pro-quo type of negotiation—"I'll do this for you, if you do this for me"—exists. This skewed boundary doesn't allow the child to develop her own healthy boundaries, her own thoughts and feelings, and her own internal resources. Acclaimed therapist Patricia Love, who has authored several books, writes: "While many [children] may have delighted in all the parental attention, on a deeper level they felt exposed and confined. They didn't feel free to be who they were or to develop at their own pace. They felt manipulated and controlled."[9]

PRIMARY PROBLEM/SECONDARY PROBLEM

Certain themes are present with the hundreds of adolescents and parents that I've worked with. The first is that the child has a **primary problem** internally: low self-esteem, poor social skills, learning difficulties, anger issues, impulsive behavior, depression, distractibility, poor self-image, a traumatic experience, or an overall emotional immaturity. These primary problems cause parents to go on high alert in an attempt to mitigate their child's struggle and alleviate symptoms. Yet the harder parents work to take away struggle, the fewer resources adolescents have to deal with stress, challenge, hardship, and rejection. Frequently, the seeds of the developmental struggles kids face through youth germinate and explode into life within the vortex of pressures in high school and beyond.

In the absence of internal resources to manage outside stressors, young people frequently choose unhealthy and external means to satiate their drive to find relief and instant gratification. They misuse/abuse alcohol and drugs; they overeat or don't eat enough; they play truant or act defiantly; they lie, become addicted to the Internet, or act out sexually; they harm themselves, isolate, think of suicide, and run away. Yet kids are gaining something from these behaviors. Drinking might assist with depression; smoking pot might soften angry feelings; cutting school might make a child feel "cool"; the Internet is a way to feel connected to others and alleviate social anxiety; sexual behavior might make a child feel wanted or loved; self-mutilation can bring temporary relief from emotional pain by incurring physical pain; and refusing food can offer the illusion of control.

It's important for parents to know that these destructive patterns are serving a purpose, because their teen doesn't know how to manage life's stressors. These behaviors are attempts—albeit flawed—to cope with or lessen suffering. Kids are further validated when their peers also engage in these behaviors, adding a social endorsement. Parents understandably react to and condemn these harming behaviors, yet criticism often only drives a further wedge between the parent and child. For a teenager with no other means of coping, these emotional soothers are lifesavers.

The critical dimension to the primary problem is that the parent–child relationship becomes a **secondary problem**. The child has to lie, avoid, and find shortcuts to maintain these habits. The parent becomes the direct target of the child's unease, the "cushion" to fall back on, the one who'll make it better. Yet the child also notices that mom and dad are becoming more and more angry at these behaviors. Additionally, it's a full-time and mentally all-consuming job for many teens to maintain one life in front of and another away from their parents' eyes. The walls between parent and child grow ever higher.

Another feature of the merged parent–child boundary is the ongoing power-struggles in the home. I remember a fellow therapist once referring to a teenage boy as "the CEO of the family." With merged boundaries, many kids assume equal footing with the adults and frequently make strategic and calculated efforts to maintain power. If a parent takes away a video game or a cell phone as a consequence of a behavior, the child will often feel angry and upset, but will act like it doesn't bother him because he doesn't want to give his parent a sense of power over him. The result is a game of negotiation.

Furthermore, when a child engages in riskier behavior, such as drug use or truancy, he often still doesn't feel a personal consequence, so it becomes a game—a way to get back at mom or dad. One adolescent was so sophisticated a liar that, to prove he was making money legally, he produced pay stubs from his pretend job, which even included social security and tax deductions. Kids go to extreme lengths to maintain their dual life, because they need a sense of self that's separate and their own. However, very rarely does it dawn on troubled adolescents that they're harming themselves—and their future, their education, and potential—with drugs, chronic lying, and failure at school. Adolescents at times feel guilty about hurting their parents, but not about harming themselves.

Today, kids feel as if their parents are holding their life in their hands, and they have to manipulate that life out of their parents' hands to have more freedom, money, cell phones, and access to a car, or to find shortcuts around school and other responsibilities. Concepts such as building trust, earning privileges, working hard, developing character, and charting their own life are difficult for children who feel entangled with their parents.

All this is to say that while their child is getting help with the *primary problem*, parents must examine the *secondary problem*. As a parent, you love your child, and want them to be successful in life. That's why your child has to take responsibility for his life and take ownership of it. You have to let her do this, so she can feel the personal consequences—both positive and negative—of her actions, the rewards and the setbacks.

I must emphasize that the problems I'm describing often emerge from very loving parents. Yet parents engaged in these entangled relationships are extremely susceptible to their children guilt-tripping them, and often work harder and harder to make their child happy.

The result is that parents lose touch with their own emotional center, intuition, thoughts, and feelings. The Parallel Process is designed to help them regain their authority by engaging in their own internal work, and be better equipped to support their child's process while rediscovering balance and harmony in the family dynamic.

DETANGLING

For many parents, fear and dependency have become the hallmarks of the bond they have with their child. Parents become frightened of setting boundaries because their children vehemently oppose them. Consequently, they're afraid their child will end up resenting them, or worse, abandon the relationship altogether. However, healthy boundaries actually provide a child with safety and comfort. Although adolescents may overtly protest and resist any limits set, explicit boundaries ultimately allow them to flourish and mature into healthy young adults. In reality, they yearn for boundaries, which give them a sense of belonging and a structure inside which they can learn and grow.

By disentangling the parent–child boundaries, parents can be responsible for their own behavior while holding kids accountable for theirs; likewise, children can develop the internal resources and coping skills necessary for navigating their own life. As psychologist Madeline Levine, Ph.D., author of *The Price of Privilege*, writes: "Autonomy, not dependency, is always the goal of good parenting."[10] The following chapters discuss such ways to disentangle: to allow teens and young adults to individuate and take charge of their own lives.

chapter 2

OWNERSHIP OF THE PROBLEM

MEREDITH

Meredith called to schedule a session in a panic, wanting to get support and clarity regarding the fine line between helping her son and enabling him. Charles, who was a young adult in college, had a series of offenses that had brought him through the court system. He'd recently been busted again, and his mother had gone into overdrive to help him out. Meredith began the session:

> Charles finally answered my calls after leaving him, like, fifteen messages. But he quickly became verbally abusive and enraged—he has had anger issues his whole life. We have never known how to deal with it . . . I mean with any boundary. He escalates to get his way. I guess he just wore us down with everything; we have no authority over him. I see now that when we gave into his demands, we were just rewarding his angry episodes. We tried so hard to make him happy—but it never worked.
>
> Now he keeps rubbing up against the law. The police busted him again, but he blames everyone else. We just got through the last episode of charges—this time he had pot and alcohol in his dorm room and he was belligerent. I fear that he is going to end up in jail. He has already been written up for shoplifting and as a minor in possession of alcohol. He is so

reckless; I am trying so hard to help him. This time Charles felt like he was targeted since he was the only one caught—he never takes responsibility. When I calmly pointed out to him that he broke the law again, and that he is on probation, he hung up on me.

I fear I am losing him. He can be the sweetest kid in the world. I know he has so much good in him, but he never sees it. We helped him get into this college; I thought this would get him on the right track. He never seems to appreciate what we do for him. I cannot keep taking this, yet I don't know what else to do. He needs help. I asked my husband, my brother, my dad to please talk to him. I am hoping Charles will listen to someone because he never listens to me. But then I am afraid my husband is too harsh on him; he can really let Charles have it . . . that is not the solution either. He refuses to go to the counseling center. He barely answers the phone when we call.

I feel he does not want our help, yet what am I supposed to do? I just want him to grow up and get through this okay. I feel so lost. The last time he had to go to court, we showed up at his dorm anyway, helped him line up a lawyer, paid the lawyer and the fines, and went to the hearing with him. I am worried that he has a bigger problem than we imagined—how do we get through to him?

When she paused, the first question I asked Meredith was, "Whose problem is this?" Charles was a young adult in college. It sounded like he obviously needed treatment for substance abuse or other behavioral or emotional issues. But the way Meredith spoke about it, it seemed that she felt the problem was her responsibility to solve. Meredith was taken aback by the question. She strongly felt that if her son had a problem, then so did she.

A critical issue in the Parallel Process is allowing the child to **own the problem**. Meredith said that she and her husband wanted Charles "to grow up and get through this," but inherent in that message was a paradox: Letting him grow up would mean letting him struggle, face adversity, and sort through his own problems and meet the consequences of his actions. And she obviously wasn't ready to let him do this. Charles needed to become invested in his own life and not be rescued by his mother. Meredith was frightened of Charles being exposed to the harsh limits of the real world (which she was already unable to prevent). In pushing his parents away, Charles wasn't seeking help; yet his parents felt compelled to fix the problem again.

Many parents don't trust their children to make good choices, and are afraid of the consequences of their negative ones, worrying that they'll be arrested, fail at school, hit bottom, and even try to commit suicide. But parents have to allow their teens to figure out the problem on their own. They can provide support, but this support is most effective through encouraging the development of internal resources, not impeding it. Naturally, parents are deeply troubled by their children's problems, but none of us can control another's life or behavior. Even if we attempt to make another person feel guilty, manipulate or placate them, at the end of the day they choose their own actions. If parents continue to take ownership of their adolescent and young adult children's problems, then the latter will continue to shirk responsibility for their own life.

It's stunning how frequently parents undermine the maturation and individuation process. I often ask them, "How responsible are you for your adolescent's life and well-being and how much responsibility does your child take?" Many reply that they put ninety percent into the relationship, and their child ten percent. Astonishingly, some even report their teen only takes one percent of the responsibility for their own education, well-being, family duties, and relationships. Ninety-nine percent is what is required to care for *infants*, not adolescents.

Yet many parents are compelled to supervise every homework assignment, call teachers frequently, sign him up for activities, clean her room, manage his emotions, help her get a job, take him to professionals, and prompt her forward with what she has to do next. Some parents have even admitted to doing the homework themselves. Parents of children in college are often calling, texting, or emailing daily to keep their child on task—even driving up to do their child's laundry and clean his dorm room on the weekends. When kids are so externally managed, they lose the opportunity to learn how to manage themselves, and adapt internally.

The parents may know they're over-involved and yet they don't know how to be in a relationship with their child in any other way. One parent told me that her child consumes a hundred percent of her mental and emotional energy. Even when he was placed out of the home in a treatment program, and his mother felt temporary relief that he was in a safe place, she experienced constant emotional preoccupation with how he was doing.

WHO IS IN CHARGE OF YOUR CHILD'S HAPPINESS?

As we've indicated, when the parent considers it his job to fix and pay for every obstacle in the child's path, then the child can redirect any problem, frustration, or inconvenience back onto the parent—including his or her *happiness*. When things don't go as hoped, teens often blame their parents for not helping them or not doing enough: "It's your fault I'm depressed; you don't let me go out at night." Or, "I look stupid in my clothes, if you bought me more clothes, I'd feel better about myself."

Many parents are deeply entrenched in this cycle of working harder and harder to make their child happy. Deftly, kids engage in all sorts of extreme behaviors to get their parents to comply with their wishes; most notably, only talking to them when they want something. In many cases, the parent–child relationship has been so reduced to parents meeting the needs of their child, and the child getting their needs met, that neither party knows how to interact differently. Parents are picking their children up, driving them around, going shopping with them, and taking them out to dinner—anything to have a relationship with them—but the consequence is that the parent is perpetually reaching to meet their child's needs and fulfill his perceived deficits.

Many entangled parents relate to their adolescents and young adults as if they were small children.

BRIT AND JERRY

Brit, who entered treatment at a wilderness program when she was sixteen, illuminated quite well the pattern she had with her parents. Her mother was a business executive and traveled frequently overseas; her father, Jerry, was her primary provider. Brit had been expelled from boarding school for repeated infractions including engaging in sexual acts on campus, selling cigarettes and Adderall, failing three subjects, and having ongoing disregard for rules. When asked about her dynamic with her parents, she described it as follows:

> My dad and mom were always sending me stuff, like every week; so I was always thinking of stuff that I needed. So, I'd know what to tell my dad on the phone. My mom sent stuff from, like, Japan and Taiwan—but my dad sent packages from home. One week, I told my dad that I needed quarters to do laundry, new jeans, and pens. He drove all over town and bought me, like, three different styles of jeans from three different stores in different shades and sizes, totaling like nine pairs of pants. He changed thirty dollars into quarters, bought three different boxes of pens from Staples, and sent another huge package.

This relationship pattern was twofold. Brit wanted to relate to her parents, so she asked for things. Her mother who was often away and her dad who missed her at home wanted to care for her. Because she was at a boarding school, they felt more removed, and were thus more compelled to provide. The underlying pattern was dependence, not empowerment, which denied Brit the ability to develop her life-skills. Mom could have asked Brit to use her allowance from the school (which parents pay into) to get quarters. Brit's dad could have asked her to save up her allowance and buy some new jeans in town and pens at the school bookstore. Yet, albeit unintentionally, they repeat-edly discouraged and undermined Brit from learning resourcefulness and self-sufficiency. When I shared with Brit my surprise that her parents had gone to such lengths to meet her needs, she shrugged: "That's nothing—my dad practically did my homework for me when I was home."

Although Brit would at times mock her father as overweight and depressed, she was deeply dependent on him. Nightly, her father or a tutor would sit next to her, supervising her homework and keeping her on task. In addition, although Brit had refined her skill in making requests of her parents, she desperately lacked self-assertion in the real world. She admitted that she'd never ordered her own meal in her life; her parents always spoke for her. She was fearful of anybody she didn't know. When she'd once babysat her younger brother and her mother had asked her to order a pizza, Brit had felt too intimidated and refused: so she and her brother had eaten cereal. She had no skills for navigating life outside the family.

It may have seemed that boarding school was a good choice for Brit—to be out of the nest and steer her own route—yet her enmeshed pattern with her parents prevailed, despite the lack of proximity. More-over, cell phones, emails, and daily texts further tethered the dependent teen to her hovering parents.

As Brit began to settle into the wilderness program, her parents' first assignment was to write a letter describing their concerns and feelings regarding Brit's behavior. Cumulatively, they wrote over thirty pages, which was whittled down to about ten. However, this assignment hardly had the intended impact. Brit liked receiving the letter but didn't take in her parent's thoughts and feelings and didn't respond to the content. She wanted them around, yet was perpetually tuning them out. This phenomenon illustrated what I call the **pursuer/dis-tancer dynamic**. Brit's dad was relentless in pursuing a relationship with Brit— instructing and lecturing her, helping her and solving her problems, and even speaking for her. Brit, however, was constantly distancing herself from him, and turning him away, though she liked knowing he was there. Jerry admitted that his kids were his whole life; he had no idea how to set a boundary, how to not be there for them or help them.

So I told Brit's parents *not* to write. She needed to feel her parents' absence—specifically her father's. Conceptually, Jerry understood this assignment; yet emotionally, he struggled greatly. Sensing this, I urged him to write just as much each week, but to put it into a journal for himself. I chose not to tell Brit initially that I'd asked her parents not to write, because I was attempting to elicit her natural response to their absence.

The week after the assignment, Brit asked whether she'd received any letters. "No," I replied. She paused for a minute and looked confused, then went on telling me about the ups and downs of her week. The following week she asked the same question, and got the same answer. At this point, she didn't ask why, but simply nodded quietly, with what I thought was slight sadness. During this time, Brit hadn't written home either. The third week, when Brit asked the same question, and I said "No" again, she wanted to know why. This wasn't like her parents, she asserted. "Something must be wrong. Why aren't they writing?" She seemed desperate. I admitted to Brit that I'd asked her parents not to write, as an assignment. She was quiet, yet seemed surprised.

"Do you know why I asked your mom and dad not to write to you?" I continued. Brit looked at me with tears in her eyes. She folded herself in her arms and cried deeply, showing her first emotion after four weeks in the wilderness. Being expelled from boarding school, being sent to the wilderness program, even getting a ten-page "impact letter" from her parents hadn't penetrated. This had. Brit looked up again: "You figured us out," she said tearfully. "You see how unhealthy we are." Not only had this intervention highlighted their mutual emotional dependency, it had prompted Brit to initiate communication, and this emotional release had finally given her the energy to communicate her real feelings. As I finished up my other sessions in the group, Brit handed me a letter to bring into the office. She now felt a natural impulse to write:

Dear Mom and Dad—

I talked with Krissy today and I had the most productive talk. I have come to see the unhealthy ways we rely on each other. The relationship we have is "enmeshed," which means that we have too much empathy, help, guilt, support, and manipulation between us. This is hurting me, because I take advantage of it, I now see how I act helpless. I sometimes feel like half a person because of your rescuing. I know I ask for it, it is helpful sometimes, yet I know I abuse it. With you, Dad, I see how we hurt each other. We try to constantly boost each other's self-esteem. We are too focused on each other and not on what really matters, which is ourselves. I realize I do nothing for myself—yet I am almost seventeen. This is an embarrassment that I hold inside. I believe if we don't rely on each other for this constant support to try to make each other happy, I think it will help me. I think what will help me the most is if you back off—even if I ask for it, don't help me. Also, don't feel like you are a bad parent because I mess up. That is my fault, not yours. Dad, I see that you are hurting yourself, too. I think you also have a problem—why don't you let me be? You feel you need to help me all the time and then I feel like I need that help—we are stuck. I continue to use and abuse your help because I know you will always be there.

I need to learn to talk for myself and live my own life. With this assignment, I think this is the first time I have not felt supported or rescued. It is hard to admit, but I'm glad. I think we can work on this issue now that we are aware of it. The reason for my actions has been to push you away—I need you to let me figure things out on my own. Yet it seems when I push you away, this only enables you to try harder. I messed up my life; it is my responsibility.

I love you, Mom and Dad,
Brit

I was astonished. After one intervention of withholding letters, the dysfunctional dynamic underneath Brit's depression, helplessness, defiance, and general disregard for boundaries and limits had come to light. She'd never taken genuine accountability for anything, because she'd put all obstacles and shortcomings at her parents' feet. As Brit gained clarity about her patterns, she experienced new life, energy, and motivation. In taking responsibility for her problems, Brit could finally feel in charge of her own problem-solving. She revealed that she was capable of amazing insight and was an excellent communicator.

Time and again, I've observed that when kids feel autonomy, they surprise you! They have talents, insights, and resources that they feel empowered to tap into. Brit recognized her part of the problem and finally felt able to take charge of her own treatment and her own life.

THE HOLE IN THE CUP

Many adolescents and young adults who are entangled with their parents are always looking externally to feel filled up—to feel happy. Clothes, drugs, technology, alcohol, money, friends, and/or freedom from their parents are what they think they need to be happy. But like the cup with the hole in it, it doesn't matter how much energy, time, money, tutors, extra privileges, professional help, and materialistic goods that parents pour into the cup, the cup is still empty. The problems still persist.

Meredith was still pouring: contacting her son, calling his college, asking her husband to phone, appeasing his anger, hiring a lawyer, paying his fines, showing up at courts, and losing her own equanimity. The hole was Charles's lack of internal resources to utilize what his parent was giving him. Only *he* could patch the hole in the cup, and actually *receive* the gifts his parents and others were giving. Brit needed a set boundary to sense her own autonomy. Even at a boarding school or in a wilderness program, nothing felt real to her because she was making her parents responsible for her life. None of the tutors, the professional help, or the specialized schools patched this hole and her problems continued unchecked. Her underlying pattern of dependence and helplessness was reinforced—notwithstanding the fact that she was living out of the home.

As we saw with Brit, what these adolescents need is to develop life-skills, such as hard work with delayed gratification, to develop internal motivation and self-discipline. To do this, they need to feel their life is their own. When young people achieve on their own, they develop esteem, confidence, and other ego-strengths. When kids work within defined boundaries to accomplish a set goal, they feel a sense of mastery, which is what ultimately brings an *internal feeling of happiness*. Parents can give a child temporary pleasure, like a present or an ice cream, but lasting happiness can only come from within the child through facing adversity and challenging oneself to achieve in life. Once parents realize the hole in the cup can only be patched by their child, they can stop tip-toeing around her, accommodating and indulging her, and can transition to supporting her through this process by letting them experience success and failure.

I remember working with a beautiful, shy, seventeen-year-old-girl who'd been out of control sexually, and was deeply ashamed of how many sexual partners she'd had. Yet she admitted to me that she wasn't sure she was ready to stop these meaningless encounters. "I feel in control and loved when I'm having sex," she said. "I know it's only temporary, but I need that attention from guys, because otherwise I feel totally repulsive." When I shared with her mother that this young woman had a poor self-image and was dependent on sexual encounters to feel accepted and beautiful, her mother couldn't understand. "I told her every day of her life that she was beautiful," she responded. "How can she have low self-esteem?"

One father complained that his son was never responsible and never appreciated what they gave him. The conversation deepened. "I keep having to re-buy him things like baseball gloves and cell phones because he loses everything," he said. When I asked him why he replaced everything, he replied: "Well, he can't play on the team if he doesn't have a glove, and I thought that was at least one positive outlet for him. How can we call him if he doesn't have a cell phone?"

Parents often complain about their child's excessive cell phone bills, yet pay for them anyway, even if they run into the thousands of dollars. "How are they going to make money to pay me back?" they ask. "They won't even do their homework. Shouldn't their education be the focus?" Cell phones are a huge source of conflict for parent and adolescents—but the issue isn't the technology, it's the pattern underlying its use. Parents keep trying to pour into the cup to give to their child: trying to give their kids self-esteem by calling them beautiful; rebuying baseball gloves so they can go to practice and feel good about themselves; rescuing them from their fines and bills. As one smug adolescent told me, "My parents are the springs on the bottom of the elevator; so I'll never hit bottom." In essence he was saying, "I'll never learn my own life-skills."

Parents can break the perpetual cycle and let their children own their problems, develop their own problem-solving skills, and be in charge of their own lives. As Robert Heinlein writes: "Do not handicap your children by making their lives easy."[11]

chapter 3

DEVELOPING INTERNAL
RESOURCES IN ADOLESCENTS

ONCE, ALL YOUNG people were able to develop internal resources and learn the life-skills essential for adulthood within the safe container of a community. Every native culture around the world had specific rites of passages for boys and girls to come of age. The transition through this life-stage was supported and acknowledged by the entire community.

Adults also knew that struggle was crucial to prepare for adulthood, which was why many rites of passage involved young people experiencing a level of suffering in order to undergo transformation. Young people would dance from sundown to sunrise, fast for days, be deprived of sleep, or go on quests alone in the wilderness. The intention of all such rites was to allow young people to leave their childhood behind and return as an adult. Through the container of these ceremonies, young people had to dig deep to find their courage and discover their intended purpose and direction in life. These rites not only ceremonially acknowledged the passage into adulthood, but more importantly they prepared these young people for adult hardships. These peoples knew that adults could not give their young men and women these skills, but that they had to develop internal resources, emotional resiliency, and strength within.

My aim is not to glorify native cultures, but to highlight the rites of passage for adolescents on which the premise of modern-day wilderness-therapy programs rest. Time and again, I've witnessed broken, depressed, despairing, self-absorbed, angry, and shut-down teens experience emotional, behavioral, and spiritual transformation through the emulation of these rites of passages. The circumstances of wilderness programs may differ from traditional ceremonies. Nonetheless, if the program is effective, the key ingredients remain: set behavioral boundaries, the container of a safe community, emotional attunement to the adolescent, and the essential thrust that struggle is imperative:

Safe Container	Set Behavioral Boundaries	Emotional Attunement	Valuing Struggle

In this chapter, I'll take liberties in speaking broadly and generally to identify the critical ingredients that promote the development of internal resources in adolescents. I lay out how vitally important the four ingredients above are in developing internal resources. I examine how, through the years, different parenting styles emphasize some ingredients at the expense of others. And I show two parenting styles at opposite ends of the spectrum to highlight what happens when some of these ingredients are omitted.

BOUNDARIES WITHOUT ATTUNEMENT

Before the 1960s in the United States, adults were in charge, institutions had authority, and communities were small enough that young people were known and supervised. Whether you grew up in small-town or rural America, or in a tight-knit urban community within a larger city, people were connected, kids were known and watched, and although adolescents still struggled and rebelled, the community provided a container with boundaries.

Kids were also out and about. Parents weren't wholly responsible for teens and emerging adults who were entering the larger world, because their neighbors, the librarians, the school, and the grocer were watching. Most parents also parented the same. Although people might have come from different cultures, ethnic groups, or socioeconomic classes, they didn't seem to have the differing parenting philosophies that exist today. Parents knew how to give consequences when a child was disrespectful, even if the child wasn't theirs. While the consequences may in some cases have been overly severe, there was a shared understanding that consequences were a necessity. This provided the container for children to undergo their own identity development, push boundaries, and explore their sense of self, within the safety of their community.

However, an essential ingredient was missing. Boundaries were set, the container was in place, and teens struggled while the community watched: yet, broadly speaking, emotional attunement was absent in the home. Parents often missed opportunities to acknowledge and empathize with their child's feelings. Most people today know that overlooking emotions can promote feelings of shame, guilt, and humiliation in kids—of being "bad." Children's "good" behavior was valued at all costs. The consequence of this parenting approach was that many kids held feelings in, shut down emotions, and harbored feelings of insecurity and inadequacy that carried into adulthood. This approach was passed down through the generations and still exists today. I call this approach of authoritarian parenting, **boundaries without attunement.** The parent lacks or withholds emotional attunement to their child, preferring to maintain behavioral boundaries: in other words, to discipline. Kids who grew up in these homes showed up in wilderness programs.

JEREMY

When Jeremy entered the treatment program he was eager and readily compliant. He was respectful, completed all his assignments, and persisted with chores—he was even cheerful. He seemed to have no "issues." Although everything appeared to be pleasant and Jeremy transitioned smoothly into the group, nobody knew what he was really thinking or feeling. Jeremy was highly uncomfortable with groups or sharing with his therapist. He often reported that he was "good" and "fine." Nothing seemed to upset him. Meanwhile, he always performed as if he was trying to get an "A" from the program.

Recognizing that Jeremy was very adaptable and behaviorally compliant, I looked deeper into the reasons for his referral, to get a better understanding of why he was placed in the program. After speaking with his parents and reading his reports, I learned that Jeremy had explosive anger issues, and a history of vandalism and blowing stuff up. When I asked him about this behavior, he downplayed it: "So what? It's not that big of a deal." Yet it was evident in talking to his parents that anger had caused a lot of discomfort. He often put fists through the wall, became verbally abusive, and threw plates and other items in the house. To deal with it, his parents had put their energy into disciplining his undesirable behavior and outbreaks.

Jeremy was also compared frequently with his older brother. "Shane never had these issues," said Jeremy's father. "We don't know what's wrong with Jeremy. We wished he could have been more like his brother. Shane didn't need to always show his emotions; he always seemed fine." What was clear was that Jeremy's parents lacked awareness and attunement to the emotions underneath his anger. They truly didn't understand him nor know what to do. In addition, they were unable to manage their own feelings. They admitted to their own issues with anger and chronic problems in their relationship (they'd been separated twice) and yet had remained together. Jeremy and his older brother, now in college, must have suffered through their parents' troubled marriage.

With time, Jeremy had learned that it was best to "hold in" his anger and work toward showing "good" behavior. Because subtler feelings of hurt, sadness, and fear weren't mirrored in the home, his parents appeared only to notice his escalated anger. Jeremy felt shame and that he was "bad" for losing control of his temper and screaming hateful things at his parents, yet he wanted them to see his hurt. As he grew up, he became more disciplined and found some healthy outlets for his energies, like football. But his explosive anger began to seep out in other ways—resulting in two arrests for making "bombs" and property damage to a nearby vacant store.

What was most critical in Jeremy's treatment was not looking at his behavior, but allowing him to feel. As his therapist, I removed his curriculum, as Jeremy seemed simply to want to jump through hoops, and suggested that what was most important was not achieving, but sharing feelings and opening up in the group. Jeremy's assignments were to disclose who he was and begin the process of identifying his *own* thoughts and feelings. Once he began to express his emotions, Jeremy began to thrive. He cried through many sessions, revealing his bottled-up feelings. He began to feel more confident in learning how to manage his emotions in appropriate ways. With time, he learned how to regulate himself emotionally and communicate his thoughts and feelings assertively to his parents, rather than act out.

In more authoritarian homes, children adapt to their parents' emotional states. Because children are so dependent on their parents, they're highly attuned to their parents' verbal and non-verbal communication. They intuitively know when dad is angry and mom is sad. These emotions can scare children and cause them to withdraw, prompt them to cheer their parents up, or respond by acting out. Jeremy acted out, but mostly in the home.

The problem with this parenting approach is that parents' emotions take precedence over the child's. When mom is sad, she doesn't own it, and as a result, children often think, "I caused mom to feel that." What Jeremy's parents were missing was emotional attunement. Jeremy had boundaries, he struggled, and he had a container at school.

Yet without attunement and validation in the home, his explosive anger still escaped, which ultimately led to arrests and treatment.

ATTUNEMENT WITHOUT BOUNDARIES

Today, the pendulum has swung from authoritarian parenting to child-centered parenting, where the parent is solely attuned to their child's emotions, needs, and wants. Permissiveness and emotional and material indulgence often hallmark this approach.

Child-centered parents focus obsessively on building their children's self-esteem. They jump at their children's whims and primarily relate to their children through fixing problems, and validating and praising them. In putting their child first, parents attempt to take away hardships and struggles by meeting the needs and wants of their child in the home, and advocating for specific requirements to help their child succeed outside it. Child-centered parents are so worried about their child's feelings that behavioral expectations and boundaries are taken away, sadness is soothed, disappointment is cheered up, and anger appeased. The primary focus is in trying to make the child happy.

With communities growing at rapid paces, extended families disconnected, and nuclear families becoming more and more isolated, the container of the safe community has dissolved. Concurrently, the boundaries within the family have been loosened. Families aren't getting their needs of closeness and intimacy met outside the home, but inside, in the parent–child relationship. This means that when a child acts out, parents often excuse the poor behavior in favor of wanting to bond and feel close with their children. Furthermore, parents don't trust what their neighbors say about their child's behavior if it's less than positive. They blame their child's teacher for a poor grade rather than hold their child accountable; in short, parents align with their children rather than join with a community effort to nurture them.

With parents pushing for their child every step of the way—like making it onto a sports team, being accepted into a private school, getting extra tutors, and professional help—parents are not only failing to let their child go out into the community to struggle and succeed (or fail) but taking on the overwhelming burden of sole responsibility for their child. Without the reinforcement of a broader community, many families suffer through parenting alone. They also fuel the narcissism and entitlement seen in so many teens.

As I've argued, we know that kids need to face adversity, dig deep, be courageous, and discover who they really are. Yet, without the trust and the container of a community, and boundaries in the home, kids are missing this vital developmental step. In the parenting approach of attunement without boundaries, boundaries are negotiable, the community container isn't safe, and struggle is mitigated. In my judgment, the journey for adolescents today is like playing Russian roulette. Lacking the essential internal resources necessary for adult life: problem-solving, delayed gratification, internal motivation, resiliency, emotional regulation, and self-discipline. Many of these kids may even feel out of control.

LILY

As soon as Lily, who'd just turned seventeen, stepped off the truck and into the wilderness-therapy program, she sat down on the side of the road: "I'm just going to wait until my mom and dad come to get me," she said. "Because this must be a mistake. My parents would never send me to a wilderness program knowingly. I am going to get dirty here, plus I can't live without my cats. I know there's a misunderstanding." When we revealed to Lily that, after she'd run away with her boyfriend, her father had felt he'd no other options than to send her to the program, she responded: "I don't know what you are talking about. My dad and I worked that out. Anyway, it's none of your business."

So Lily sat at the side of the road until it got cold and we made a fire for her and helped set up her campsite. She was uncooperative and utterly disbelieved she was in a program, because up to this point there'd been no limits. She had a way of "working everything out" with her parents, which in essence meant she could talk her way around anything, because in her mind everything was negotiable. She'd applied this philosophy to high school as well, and had been "on medical leave" (i.e. not attending classes) for four months due to her depression and lack of internal motivation. She had no hobbies or passions, and lacked any motivation and self-discipline. Lily had been supposed to take online courses while her parents were at work, but she never seemed to get to it. She did, however, spend hours online, chatting with her boyfriend. She'd become steeped in lying, which had escalated into her running away with him. They'd disappeared for two days, taking an eight-hour train ride covering three states.

At the same time, Lily felt she was very close to her parents, especially her father. She told him *almost* everything, she said, and thought the world of him. She would light up when talking about him and called him "the funniest guy on earth." Her mother described Lily and her father as "cut from the same cloth," so deeply did they understand each other. It was very hard for him to say "No" to Lily. Her parents had rules, but never enforced them; so Lily learned that rules don't really mean anything.

At the program, Lily attempted to run away from her group, but didn't get very far away in the Utah desert. She soon realized that she wasn't going to get "rescued" by her parents and fell into despair. She assumed that if she became more and more dramatic, someone would rescue her. Yet she discovered that the drama only prolonged her process. Eventually, she wrote her parents a loving, but very angry, letter. When her father read about her attempt to run away, he almost jumped out of his skin; he fought mightily not to come and pick her up. He knew that Lily was out of control and that nothing would change if he got her out; yet he was deeply worried about her emotional state and felt powerless not to be able to cheer her up, tell her a joke, or take her out to sushi and a movie—their favorite thing to do together. Lily's father was constantly in emotional turmoil with his daughter out of the home. Yet he felt it was the only option to keep her safe. Her mother was equally distraught.

Lily's therapy consisted of holding firm boundaries, where the only forward movement in the program came through completing each task and earning advancement to the next level. This meant that she spent three weeks on the first level (which usually takes seven days) because it took her so long to demonstrate basic self-care, such as eating her meals, staying hydrated, following the rules, keeping her pack and gear organized, and making her first fire. Lily had been operating in an adult world with a lot of freedoms, but she lacked the skills of many younger children, such as looking after herself and her belongings, and following basic rules.

After a lot of struggle, and many periods of giving up, Lily eventually advanced to the next level. Her eyes glowed and she felt on top of the world. Facing adversity and overcoming an obstacle is an enormous boost to esteem and confidence—especially when no one is there to rescue you and you're able to do it by yourself. Lily loved to process her feelings—she could do it for hours! Yet she had few skills to solve problems and complete tasks. Her therapy continued with firm boundaries and little processing. She had to learn to struggle, solve problems, and dig deep.

Eventually, through many dramatic ups and downs, Lily made it through all the phases. Later, she recalled that her wilderness program had been a great blessing, one of the best experiences of her life. Although it was still a long and strenuous road for her parents to learn to set limits, Lily clearly thrived as a result of the boundaries, the support of her group, and natural consequences. Every day, these boundaries gave her choices, enhancing her feeling of personal empowerment. In attuned parenting without boundaries, kids feel close to their parents but are very dependent on them because they are not used to the rules and consequences of the real world; they are only used to negotiating with their parents. Lily had a special bond with her dad, yet she lacked the internal resources and life-skills needed to successfully navigate high school.

ADOLESCENT TREATMENT PROGRAMS: THE NEW CONTAINER

For adolescents who've gotten off-track developmentally and parents who've lost boundaries and attunement in the home, adolescent treatment programs in essence recreate the needed container. In the four treatment programs I've worked at, and in the countless others I'm familiar with, adolescents have to work though stages, levels, and phases within which they struggle with set criteria until they attain a level of mastery and achieve the next phase or level on their own. They do this with the help of a therapist who attunes emotionally to the child. A peer group and larger community normalize the experience and provide support through the process. Within these phases, young people form internal resources that allow them to motivate themselves, set goals themselves, delay gratification, learn self-awareness, regulate their emotions, communicate effectively, and become resilient.

In the container of treatment centers, kids can fail and learn to stand up, pick up the pieces, and continue to charge forward safely. They're not rescued; the staff knows what these kids are capable of achieving. They may not do it the first, second, or even the tenth time; but they will. What the community communicates is that it's safe to struggle, and that it sees the struggle and honors it. With this, kids learn that it's safe to resume their emotional development. Just as in native cultures, these programs know that kids can only develop strength within. We cannot give it to them, and we cannot make it better.

CREATING A CONTAINER IN THE HOME

Often, a matrix of clinical, behavioral, and emotional issues propels struggling teens out of the home and into a treatment program. To reset, they need individual clinical attention and to be removed from old, self-destructive habits and their dysfunctional dynamics with their parents, peers, and others. Yet for kids still at home, or in anticipation of the adolescent who's currently in treatment and about to come home, parents can learn to create a container in the house. It's problematic for parents to send their child to treatment and bring him home expecting different results if changes are not also underway at home.

Before parents attempt to reinstate these changes, they first need to assess how they were operating on the attunement–boundaries continuum before their child went to treatment:

All attunement _____ balanced _____ all boundaries
no boundaries   attunement with boundaries   no attunement

Parents need to examine their old parenting style honestly. If they were inclined to attunement, they need to focus wholly on limits and boundaries; likewise, parents who knew how to set limits yet lacked attunement need to focus wholly on emotional attunement. Moms and dads frequently differ in their approaches and each needs to counterbalance and compensate for their own natural tendencies. (For example, in some families, mom now has to set the limits, and dad can only listen and reflect.)

Creating a container may be the hardest step because it involves many adults having a shared understanding about the importance of these elements. First, it involves mom and dad, or step-parents, grand-parents, aunts, and uncles coming together to build a container for this child. In addition, teachers, school officials, therapists, tutors, coaches, and other adults in the child's life must all work in concert. Struggling or at-risk teens are proficient at compartmentalizing—telling adults different stories, splitting up parents or pitting one against the other—and unhappy kids want to focus on controlling others rather than developing internal control. When the container is set up, the adults are unified. This minimizes splitting and can sustain struggle, failure, and even relapse upon returning home. For such young people, building these internal skills is an ongoing process, and parents should expect setbacks. Yet parents cannot do the work for kids; they can only create safety, consistency, and follow-through.

The container allows three other elements to come together: behavioral boundaries and expectations, emotional attunement, and valuing struggle. Follow-through and consistency with these three is arduous, and takes time and ongoing practice. In the following chapters, I provide specific ways to stay emotionally close and connected to your child while employing these essential elements. Parents can learn assertive communications skills, accountability, reframing, self-awareness, and reflective listening—all skills to navigate this new approach, called **balanced parenting.**

chapter 4

BALANCED PARENTING

PARENTING IS AN ongoing balancing act between the parents' and child's needs. Of primary importance is meeting the physical needs of children: feeding and nourishing them; keeping them safe (e.g. dressed, bringing him or her to school, and providing a home). Many families do this naturally and instinctively, and most are able to meet these needs no matter how difficult their circumstances may be.

Equally important as satisfying the physical needs of children, however, is providing for their emotional and behavioral requirements. Knowing how to respond to these, however, is harder and not always instinctive. In setting boundaries and attuning themselves to their children's emotions, parents often repeat the patterns of their own parents or swing to an opposing parenting philosophy as described in the previous chapter. What is essential is that parents balance behavioral boundaries with emotional attunement.

BEHAVIORAL BOUNDARIES

Boundaries are placed when parents decide that a behavior has crossed a line. For example, they might decide that a temper tantrum, hitting a sibling, or cursing at a parent, lying about school, getting an "F," or being caught with marijuana is unacceptable. When a parent deter-

mines a behavior has gone too far, he or she will stop and communicate with the child or teen and set a boundary. Behavioral boundaries
are held or enforced through giving consequences, like leaving a play-
ground early, asking a child to take a break in his room, or taking away
a privilege like use of a cell phone or an allowance. These consequences
teach kids that there are limits in life, that a cause has an effect. Boundaries also give kids choices. When there's no escape or shortcut around
a boundary, when the external circumstances are firm and intact, kids
need to adapt internally, to develop their own resourcefulness and
adjust their behavior. Madeline Levine writes:

> There are many reasons for parents to set limits on children to promote
> safety, responsibility, thoughtfulness—but perhaps the most compelling
> one is that adolescents simply don't have the tools, prefrontal cortex devel-
> opment, the judgment to consistently and appropriately regulate them-
> selves.[12]

With this in mind, it's more effective to set boundaries clearly and
authoritatively, without involving emotions. One shouldn't guilt-trip
the child, using a judgmental or critical tone of voice. One should state
firmly: "If you do ——, the consequence will be ——." You should
expect children to make mistakes; when they do, it's not the end of
the world. When parents know this attitude is part of the job, they're
able to hold a boundary without adopting an "I'm so disappointed
in you" manner. With a non-reactive approach, kids won't become
tangled up in mom or dad's emotion. Instead, they'll be forced to look
at their own behavior. But for parents, it is often easier not to enforce
boundaries because holding children accountable can create tension
in the parent–child relationship; however, it's critical to note that this
happens at the child's expense. All these small tensions of holding
boundaries can keep a child on course developmentally because they
reinforce self-management skills and individuation.

Inherent in enforcing boundaries is struggle. Developmental psychologist Erik Erikson identified eight stages of ego-development. At the heart of every stage, he suggested, was struggle. In adolescence, the struggle is between identity and role confusion.[13] Identity develops through the trials and errors of a young person thrusting her inner world into the outer one, while receiving feedback. As she develops competency and attains mastery by achieving goals, she gains confidence and esteem, while also honing her sense of self. In healthy development, noted Erikson, adolescents become more aware of who they are as individuals, rather than being solely identified with where they come from and how they were raised. They start to form their own opinions and beliefs, and begin to separate from their families of origin and enter the larger world and society. This happens through continually pushing up against boundaries and struggling, and is what we mean by individuation.

Long before he became a therapist, a colleague of mine worked on a cattle ranch. He noticed that during the first days the cows were taken to an enclosed pasture, they stuck to the perimeter, using their bodies to push up against the fence while they grazed. When my friend asked the rancher about this behavior, the latter told him that the cows would do this for the first few weeks in order to see if the fence was secure. Each and every day, the rancher and his crew would be in the pasture, fixing any broken parts of the fence, until all was repaired. "Even though the best-tasting alfalfa is in the middle of the field," the rancher told my friend, "the cows won't touch it, until they feel safe. If there's an opening in the fence, they can get out and would be unprotected from the dangers outside, or a predator could come inside. Once the cows know the perimeter is secured, they'll come in to the center for the good stuff."

This metaphor stuck with my friend in his years of working with teens. Just like the cows, adolescents push up against limits to learn where the boundaries are. Cows are sure to find any insecure parts in the fence; kids, too, are adept at spotting any "weak link"—whether quarreling parents or loopholes in the school system, or any other inconsistency. I repeatedly watched adolescents in wilderness assess which instructors had more "authority" so they could identify those who might be a "weak link."

Like a caring, intuitive rancher, parents must also continue to hold firm boundaries, repairing any weak links so their children can gain the benefits of being on safe pasture. If through testing limits and boundaries, kids find that the boundary is movable, they become confused and anxious. When boundaries are negotiable or limits not clearly defined, adolescents put more energy into moving or manipulating them, rather than adapting internally.

Conversely, when children know their boundaries, they're more able to engage in healthy and dynamic relationships with their parents, because they no longer have to worry about their own safety. Kids switch their energy to work within a system, family, school, and so on. They feel secure enough in their relationship with their parents to explore new ideas, beliefs, and life experiences, and confident enough in their own emerging individuality to take calculated risks in the community and begin the process of forming their own separate self, developing internal resources and resiliency. Unfortunately, many adolescents today are missing the Eriksonian life-lessons and aren't developing their own identity and esteem. Young people face a rude awakening when they enter the adult world and realize boundaries are set and unyielding.

EMOTIONAL ATTUNEMENT

Emotional attunement is mirroring back to a child that you see what they're feeling. When a child is angry, sad, frustrated, scared, or worried, a parent can validate the emotion: "I can see that you're scared of starting a new school," or "You seem sad about the fight with your friend." This mirroring communicates to a child that it's okay to have emotions, positive or negative. The message is: "I see you." *What kids want most is to be seen and heard by their parents.*

The primary premise of attachment theory, as developed by John Bowlby, is "emotional attunement."[14] Parents attune to an infant and toddler by meeting their physical and emotional needs, which helps to ensure they feel safe in the world and creates the foundation for their ability to develop trust in relationships. Again, most parents meet their child's needs for food, shelter, and clothing, yet emotional cues are often harder to read and respond to—"Do I buy him the toy to make him happy or say 'no' and let him struggle?" Bowlby's attachment theory suggests that one responds to emotional cues through mirroring and attuning, and not fixing. Daniel Siegel, a specialist on neurobiology and attachment, writes:

> When a parent's initial response is to be attuned to his child, the child feels understood and connected to the parent. Attuned communications give the child the ability to achieve an internal sense of balance and supports her in regulating her bodily states and later her emotions and states of mind with flexibility and equilibrium. These experiences of attuned connections and the balance they facilitate enable the child to achieve a sense of coherence within her own mind.[15]

In attuned communication, parents validate the child's emotions, internal reality, and sense of self. Tuning-in requires identifying the emotion and reflecting it back, so the child feels seen and heard: "You sound upset, can you tell me what you are feeling," or, "I can see that you really want that toy, can you tell me about it?" In simply saying "yes" or "no," the parent can miss the emotional attunement. Through attunement, mirroring, and validation, parents not only assure kids that it's safe to feel emotions, but moreover, develop a fundamental component in parent–child attachment through the establishment of an emotional connection.

Parents frequently become frustrated with their children's emotions and unintentionally communicate that feelings aren't okay by trying to stifle them: "Stop crying," or "Stop whining." Instead, parents can communicate two messages at once: "I want to understand what you're feeling, but it's very hard when you're whining and crying." Or: "You sound sad; I want to listen when you're calmer." This message validates feelings and encourages the sharing of them; more importantly, however, it lets kids know that whining and crying aren't effective ways to communicate.

Other parents move too quickly toward comforting emotions. This again, misses the attunement, which is often confused with comforting. It's understandable that parents typically want to soothe "negative" emotions; yet it's unhelpful in the long run because it interrupts the ability for kids to "self-soothe." Take for example the following statements: "I'm sure you'll be fine when you start your new school," or "I'm sure you and your friend will work out the conflict." These may be simple, seemingly harmless comments; however, over time they can be detrimental. A child learns her feelings are invalid if they're repetitively overlooked. *Validating an emotion means allowing your child to feel it.* For example, "It *is* scary to start a new school, how do you think you'll cope with it?" "It *is* uncomfortable to have fights with friends, how are you feeling about it?"

I taught this concept of emotional attunement and validation at a staff training, and it was striking to me how a subtle shift in response can elicit deeper sharing. I asked staff to pair up in dyads, where each had a turn at telling the other some stressor from the week working with kids in the wilderness. In the first round, the listener had to "make it better." So for example, when one member of staff said, "I got really overwhelmed with X student who was always opposing everything I said," the other's response was, "I'm sure you did a great job; these kids can be challenging." Though this statement may seem supportive, the conversation was brief and prevented any deeper sharing.

In the second round, one staff member would tell the same story, but the other member had to attune emotionally and validate. So, in response to, "I got really overwhelmed with X student who was always opposing everything I said," he or she would reply, "That sounds difficult and frustrating, how did you handle it?" This response led to a deeper conversation, where the sharing and listening led to a feeling of connection. Though it took many staff some time to sort out the difference between "making it better" and emotional attunement and validation, the sharers reported that when the listeners tried to make the situation better, they felt their emotions were being invalidated. When they were "heard" by the other, however, the exchange was more satisfying, and actually brought relief.

As a parent myself, I'm constantly reminding myself to validate and attune. In the intense ups and down of small children's emotions, it's easy to overlook feelings. For example, my daughter misplaced a book that she wanted to read in bed and quickly went into a full-blown melt-down. At first, I started to get mad at her reaction and that only escalated her further. So I stopped and said, "You seem so upset and I know how upset I feel when I lose things." She immediately calmed down, because instead of saying, "stop feeling," I'd validated her feeling. I then said, "Screaming about it isn't helping; what would you like to do about it?" She calmly asked me, "Mommy, will you help me look for my book?" So we looked for the book together and found it in another room.

When parents don't acknowledge fear, sadness, hurt, and frustration in a child, and instead try to assuage or quell the emotion, they're interrupting their child's ability to solve their own problems. All of us, at any stage of our lives, have the ability to shift into and out of emotions naturally. When kids are taught, compassionately, to stay with their emotions, they're given the opportunity to learn to regulate them, as opposed to being impulsive, overly reactive, or trying to escape them. For parents truly to validate and acknowledge their children's emotions, they need to be in touch and comfortable with their own. This critical part of the Parallel Process is outlined in the following chapters.

BALANCED PARENTING

Parents love their children unconditionally. However, it's feasible to be both emotionally attuned to your children while still maintaining boundaries and discipline. Limits discourage a child's poor behavior, not her emotion; likewise acknowledging your child's emotions doesn't mean dismantling limits. The trick is finding the balance.

When children show poor behavior—such as biting or hitting, having a tantrum, stealing, lying, or playing truant—parents can do both: "It's *not* okay to hit your sister. I see that you're sad because she has the toy you want. I'd like you to take a time-out and rest on your bed first." Or: "I see how angry you are that you failed your test, and I want to hear more about what you're feeling. Yet lying is not an acceptable response. As a result, you'll have the consequence of no computer tonight." Or: "It must feel so painful to be rejected by your friend. I hope you feel safe enough to share more with me. Nevertheless, stealing from your friend as a response comes with consequences."

Anger is equally as authentic as happiness on the spectrum of emotions. When a child acts out his anger—such as by throwing a toy or punching a hole in the wall—a parent can validate the feeling while invalidating the behavior, by holding a boundary: taking the toy away or asking the teen to pay for the hole in the wall. Furthermore, the parent can reward a child or teen for taking steps to experience the anger without harming himself or others. To be a fully integrated adult, kids need to learn to feel and stay with their emotions, while also knowing that all behaviors have consequences. When kids know there are consequences for their behavior, both positive and negative, they realize they have choices. This can occur even at very young ages. They will see that hard work will earn privileges and trust, while disrespect and lying will lose both. We must allow our children to develop the life-skills they'll need in the adult world.

Yet many parents feel they're being "mean" when they impose a boundary or a limit, and many parents intentionally steer away from limits, discipline, or simply saying "no." Author Alfie Kohn endorses such a philosophy and identifies any type of parental limit as a "love withdrawal."[16] He describes any boundary pejoratively, as controlling the child through a reward or punishment. He argues that imposing any limit is "conditional love" or any consequence is "repackaged punishment."[17] Parents have an understandable fear of not wanting to create anxiety, guilt, and shame in their child—something they may remember from their own childhood. Yet, it's essential for parents to separate out feelings and behavior, so their children receive consequences for poor behavior and not for their feelings and emotions.

Pace Kohn, I believe limits send a message of love and parental care. When a parent has set a time for the child to go to bed, the message is: "Sleep is very important, and I'm going to make sure you get enough sleep every night." When a parent establishes a curfew, the message is: "I care where you are, and I'm going to wait by the door to make sure you're home at a safe hour." Boundaries also allow you, the parents, to send the message: "I'm going to hold you to a higher level of behavior because I know you're capable of it." Just like in a traditional rite of passage, you're communicating: "I know you can do this; I know you have it in you. I believe in your strengths." On the other hand, when parents rescue kids from limits, they're inadvertently saying: "I know you need help, so I'll help you with your chore, homework, or whatever the expectation is. I'm not sure if you're capable of doing this yourself." In this way, kids learn to depend upon the parent, rather than on themselves.

Child-centered perspectives overlook the possibility that one can honor positive behavior and discourage negative behavior in a way that also acknowledges, validates, and nurtures a child's sense of self. Boundaries foster children's ability to make healthy choices while coming to understand that unhealthy choices carry consequences. I sometimes wonder if in the interest of protecting their children, parents have become so attuned to and concerned about their child's emotions, needs, and wants, that they've lost touch with the essential truth that life is a series of hardships. Whether we're navigating high school, succeeding in college, pursuing a career, or starting a family, our lives consist of challenges. Children will be teased, rejected, or put down—which is why they need to first struggle within the home with limits and consequences to develop internal mastery. When children are raised without limits or behavioral boundaries, many lack drive, motivation, and internal control. When kids learn that life is "easy" in the home while meeting constant impediments outside the home, chances are they won't successfully launch into adulthood.

THE FALLACY OF SELF-ESTEEM BUILDING

The self-esteem movement has fueled child-centered perspectives, which focus on trying to make kids feel happy and good, rather than encouraging them to challenge themselves to uncover their own talents. For example, many sports teams now give all kids trophies at the end of the season, rather than acknowledging the most talented, most improved, or most spirited teammate. When kids put in average effort and still get a trophy, or parents are perpetually bolstering, praising, and validating, kids in my experience feel worse because they didn't *earn* the praise.

Self-esteem has two key components, which mirror the premise of balanced parenting.

1) Knowing you are loved for who you are, regardless of what you do. This is modeled by how your caregivers treat you and is learned from infancy on.
2) Feeling competent and achieving at tasks, gained through applying and engaging yourself in real-world activities such as sports, school, music, art, or other tasks in which problem-solving, independence, and autonomy are engaged.

While parents cannot *give* their child self-esteem, no matter how hard they try, they can promote its development by showing unconditional love, while also actively supporting real-life activities that allow for the opportunity to succeed and fail. Parents can also set up containers within the home where kids can apply themselves and develop internal resources, through earning privileges for healthy choices and facing consequences for poor ones.

When kids master one environment, they demonstrate that they're ready to move toward more independence in a new environment. Just like a baby develops enough self-control in a crib to graduate to a big bed, a teen can responsibly master his own chores in the house to earn the ability to get a job outside the home. When teens build the internal skills to navigate their responsibilities, they're showing that they're ready to move into a bigger environment with more freedom, but also more responsibilities. Unfortunately today, kids push for more and more freedoms without the emotional maturity or internal skills to handle the level of responsibility. Parents are enabling this by providing children with freedom that should be earned rather than received through manipulation or entitlement.

Today, kids want cars, clothes, cell phones, money, and computer access—and often get them because parents feel they're old enough, or they win through negotiation. But parents aren't attuning to their emotional maturity. Many seventeen-year-olds may be emotionally more like thirteen-year-olds, especially if substance abuse is involved. Once kids rely on external means to numb themselves, they're stunting their emotional growth, which can manifest itself in a variety of ways—such as excessive watching of television, spending too much time on the computer, playing endless video games, and abusing drugs and alcohol . . . or even reading too many romance novels. I once worked with a girl who read romance novels roughly twelve hours a day. She wasn't engaging in the world, she was escaping it.

Internal feelings of happiness and esteem are achieved through struggle, hard work, and reaching goals. This process is exemplified daily in wilderness-therapy programs. In the wilderness, achieving anything is a process that requires perseverance with delayed gratification. Whether you're making a fire without matches to stay warm or cook dinner, hiking cross-country to a new campsite to find water, or packing up in the morning with frozen hands, you're required to be patient and acknowledge *process*. The paradox is that teens in such situations have none of their "wants" met, yet they toil daily as a group and eventually feel the rewards and outcomes of their efforts: a hot burrito, a warm drink, a fire to sit by and rest their tired legs, a new campsite near a creek, and internal happiness.

Hard work can take many forms, whether they're chores in the home to earn money, discipline on a sports team, academic diligence, charity work, participating in a club, pursuing personal hobbies, attending practices, doing recitals, completing homework—these build life-skills. Without these, adolescents who are used to negotiating boundaries and manipulating limits, rather than their mastering their internal environment, are extremely vulnerable in the adult world. By continually seeking instant gratification and calculating short cuts, they don't build up the esteem, confidence, and internal skills necessary for adult life.

In summary, parents can find the middle ground through having behavioral boundaries *with* emotional attunement. Balanced parenting attempts to emulate the core principles that exist in rites of passage and integrate all these essential ingredients into one parenting approach. Struggling to achieving mastery of a skill or a task within set boundaries, with emotional attunement, and within a container, builds confidence, esteem, and self-discipline; provides for the regulation of emotion, resiliency, and internal motivation; and allows a child to delay gratification, set goals, and solve problems.

part 2

THE PARALLEL PROCESS

chapter 5

THE PARENT PROCESS

THE GOAL OF the Parallel Process is for parents to regain their footing, learn and grow so they can meet their son or daughter with new awareness, insight, perspective, and appreciation, in a new place. The Parallel Process can safeguard all the emotional work your child is doing in treatment by learning how to integrate these new skills into the family. Why this is necessary is shown by Jeff and Diane.

JEFF AND DIANE

Jeff and Diane called me after their son Tom was placed in a wilderness program for young adults with addictions. During the first session, Diane described the history of Tom's issues and struggles:

> Tom is my middle child and he was always a fairly easy child to raise, in the sense that he didn't seem to have too many tantrums or behavioral problems. He is very bright; but he was diagnosed early on as having ADD, which I think affected his maturity and esteem. Through the years, he was able to maintain his grades enough by acing his tests; he managed to graduate from high school, and he was accepted to a reputable college. He seems to have a photographic memory, yet I am not sure how much he truly applied himself. What we now see is that he is a skilled manipulator,

making it seem as though he is on top of everything, though in reality the only thing he is in control of is shaping his image; underneath we see how void and lost he is. He is a savvy kid, fooling everyone, including himself.

Although I was thrilled about his college acceptance, I was worried because he was always disorganized, he lacked study skills, and he was still behind socially and emotionally—compared to many of his peers. Yet, he had this façade that all was "fine" and I guess I fell for it. There were periods in high school where he admitted to depression and he was placed on medication. And during his freshman year in college he asked for medication again; this was in addition to the ADD medication he has been on since middle school. In the fall of his freshman year, he managed to pass all of his classes, but by the winter it was evident that he was seriously depressed. We soon learned that he was using alcohol and pot, and abusing his medications, including Ritalin and Xanax. He actually sought out extra prescriptions from healthcare providers near the college, while also having his psychiatrist at home. We finally got a call from the school about his poor attendance—this was when it was clear that things were out of control.

Because he screened our calls, we drove up to see him at school and discovered that the problem was much bigger than we imagined. We found him passed out on his bed. Once we located his roommate, Ryan, we were finally able to get him to talk—since he had just been protecting Tom up to that point. Ryan shared that Tom had not gone to classes for weeks. He stayed up all night drinking and smoking pot, and slept all day. Yet what was further disturbing was that he was not even socializing or going to parties, he was isolating in his room. We now learned that he is also addicted to gaming and he played for ten hours straight every night. He has this elaborate cyberworld. I think Ryan became the only person he related to; it was like he was living in a cocoon of gaming and alcohol. It is as though his house of cards finally fell in on him. Ryan felt that he was becoming reckless—he even worried about suicide. At one point, Ryan encouraged him to go to the counseling center and Tom refused, he was shut down emotionally and apathetic. With the help of an educational consultant, and thank God, his roommate Ryan, who was able to talk straight to him, he agreed to go to a wilderness program and take a medical leave from his college. It was frightening to us how little we knew.

Diane and Jeff felt relief that Tom had agreed to go to treatment; they also expressed confidence in his wilderness program. Nevertheless, they were troubled to learn about Tom's dual life. "Tom wrote us a letter of accountability," Diane said, "and although we are grateful that he was so honest, we were deeply shocked to learn how secretive he was."

Jeff continued: "He was always emotionally introverted, but now we realize how much he was covering up. Tom wrote that he began abusing pot and alcohol freshman year—through an older kid on the soccer team. His use significantly increased in the last two years of high school. He also sold pot and his Ritalin—I guess to pay for his addiction. He admitted to smoking pot daily and had a ritual of doing it late in the night in his room by himself—to chill out. He felt he needed it to sleep. He would keep the window open, the fan on, and wore his 'weed clothes.' He has even tried meth, ecstasy, and cocaine. Although we have never been aware of a girlfriend, he also revealed that he is sexually active."

"We are horrified. How could we have been so naïve?" Diane added. "I definitely suspected him being drunk or high at times, but I guess I believed him—it never occurred to me that he could have lied like this. He always said the right thing and there he was, still acing his tests; so I guess that was all I needed to think everything was okay. I knew all kids experimented with drugs and alcohol a little."

Unfortunately, extremely bright kids who struggle with mental-health issues and lack the self-management skills needed to make healthy choices can also be very savvy at deceiving others. This certainly was the case for Tom. As Tom settled into his wilderness program, where we knew he was safe, I switched the focus to Diane and Jeff to understand more of their history.

Diane was an elementary school teacher, and the primary caretaker of Tom, his younger brother Brett, and his older sister Jenna, who was a recent college graduate. Diane managed and organized the family. Emotionally, she was on an even keel, even stoic. She further revealed that her mother had passed away, and had been an alcoholic, indicating a history of addictions in the family. Diane still cared for her aging father; yet she described their relationship as "emotionally cold."

Diane revealed that, although she always felt close to her middle child, she "never knew what Tom was thinking and feeling." When asked further about this, Diane disclosed that she had very little awareness of her *own* feelings, too. "I guess I don't really tune in to my own feelings; it just seems too daunting, too unknown, too overwhelming." She then admitted to feeling unsure of how to proceed with Tom: "He's become so manipulative, angry, and passive aggressive. I have no idea how to talk to him anymore. I'm so grateful that our consultant was able to intervene and could confront him because I just feel lost. It's almost like I don't even know who he is anymore." When I probed further, she stated: "I feel completely shut down inside and frozen. I don't know how to talk about these feelings with anyone."

Jeff was much more the emotional parent. He was an entrepreneur and was frequently immersed in huge projects, which involved a lot of travel. He, too, had problems organizing himself—like Tom—and, at times, he drank too much. Because he wasn't home as much as he would have liked, Jeff always made time to "connect" with his children. Brett loved his time with his father and Jenna always felt a close connection with him; but Jeff repeatedly felt rejected by Tom. The latter was chronically irritated with his dad and seemed to want nothing to do with him.

Because Jeff was more emotional, he'd feel hurt and show his frustration when Tom pushed him away. "I knew Tom was emotionally withdrawn and held a lot in," Jeff told me, "but all he did was say he was 'fine' and would share little more. This was maddening for me, because I wanted to know how school was, how soccer was, how his friends were. I would get angry, yell, and lecture him, which I always regretted. Then I would praise him. I learned from his recent letter that he especially hated this because he felt he did not earn the praise. Truthfully, I don't know how to relate to him; the harder I try, it seems the more he pulls away. It's all I think about."

Jeff felt lost, too. Although Jeff and Diane were finally learning more about their son through his letters and assignments, it seemed this information about Tom's hidden life was unraveling the family. Jeff was tense and unable to sleep; Diane was shut down, and they could barely talk to each other about Tom because they were too locked into their own patterns. They were even questioning their marriage, since they felt there was no glue left in their relationship: it was too exhausting to relate; it was easier to just avoid each other. Meanwhile, Brett was only fourteen and had no idea where Tom was. Diane and Jeff hadn't spoken to any friends or family yet about Tom's placement in treatment; they simply didn't know what to say. As Tom began the process of addressing his addictions and emotional withdrawal in order to function better as an adult, the family's functioning seemed to be getting worse. Their home-life felt chaotic, as everything they understood to be true was dismantled.

Jeff and Diane shared one other significant event in Tom's history. Though, initially, Tom and Diane didn't see its relevance, when they were asked to trace back to events that impacted Tom, both parents simultaneously commented on it. As a small child, Tom had been deeply attached to his grandfather, Jeff's father, who lived next-door when Tom was young. Tom would visit him every day. "They loved to play Lego and trains," said Jeff, "and would spend hours together after school and on the weekends. It was very sweet. When Tom was only seven, shortly after he came home from my dad's house, my dad had a sudden heart attack and died instantly. It was devastating for everybody. We assumed Tom would be distraught; however, when we told him, he showed no emotion. He was like a shell. This was when we really saw his pattern of emotional withdrawal start. We did not know what to do. He has refused to talk about his grandfather ever since."

THE PARENTS' PATTERNS

Tom was nineteen years old when he was placed in a young-adult wilderness-therapy program to sort out his emotional issues and substance abuse problems. Though it was painful for them to admit, Jeff and Diane couldn't control whether Tom became sober or whether he finished college. They couldn't control his depression. At their core, they felt powerless. Moreover, Diane and Jeff were unsure of where they'd gone wrong with Tom, and didn't know how to proceed. Learning about all the lies, they didn't know if they could ever trust him again.

Tom's therapist in his program explained to Jeff and Diane that their son was in a safe container, intended for him to struggle within. Breaking his pattern of emotional withdrawal and becoming sober would take time, as would applying himself to healthy pursuits. This was Tom's process; in the meantime, Diane and Jeff knew they needed help. They were nervous about saying the wrong thing; they only wanted to help—to do whatever they could for Tom. Yet at home, they felt despair. Life felt unmanageable; it was impossible to continue normally knowing Tom was suffering. They needed their own support.

Through engaging in a parallel process, Tom and Diane found choices: to do their own internal work to enhance their self-awareness; to own their patterns and choose to relate differently with their son. This wouldn't fix Tom, but they could shift to a healthier place to support him and feel more at ease themselves. They could also help safeguard the emotional work Tom was doing by becoming more aware as a family. Jeff and Diane could do their part.

Courageously, Tom opened up in his letters and disclosed more about himself. Though he reached out, Jeff and Diane didn't know how to respond. My first assignment as their therapist, guiding them through a parallel process, was to ask Diane to keep a "feelings journal." I requested her to jot down three emotions each day in a small notebook. I told her she could write more if she felt like it, but that she had to provide a minimum of three each day. Diane would have to stop what she was doing, attune to her own emotions, and note a feeling—tiredness, relief, embarrassment, tension, calmness, sadness, agitation, feeling overwhelmed, or spaced out: she just had to write whatever she was feeling. I asked not to judge her emotion, react to it, or try to change it, but merely attune to it, become aware of it.

The premise of the assignment was that Diane would access her own emotions, which could in turn allow her to be more emotionally available for her son. Though on the surface this may appear to have been a simple assignment, Diane found it extremely challenging. First off, she often didn't even know what she was feeling. She was then fearful of opening that valve lest she be inundated by negative emotions. She'd worked her whole life to find order and keep unwanted feelings at bay. I was asking her to disrupt this deeply entrenched strategy. Though the assignment was difficult and painful, Diane also showed courage in attempting it. I further suggested that they "check in" as a family in the evenings to offer emotional support to each other. Diane told me that this was too much initially for her. However, after a few weeks of journaling feelings, she was willing to attempt this.

Jeff first needed to address his own feelings of guilt and failure, which were causing his insomnia. He felt that he'd been present more for Jenna when she was young. When Tom had turned two, Jeff was often on the road because of his work, and he felt this had contributed to his inability to build a foundation with Tom. Moreover, as an entrepreneur, Jeff was always fixing problems—whether at home or work. His pattern was to work at the problem until it was resolved; he was extremely uncomfortable with being still, listening, and inaction. With Tom, Jeff was always trying to connect, praise, fix, or attempt to make him feel better or give him what he wanted. He was always *doing*; he didn't know how to just *be*. All the while, Tom resisted his dad's help. Jeff didn't carry the same anxiety with Brett and Jenna, since they normally welcomed his efforts. Yet it was clear that in all his relationships Jeff struggled with being emotionally present.

When I told Jeff that Tom's problem was not his to fix, he said that he felt powerless and restless. I also reminded Jeff that relationships exist in the present; he always had the power to relate differently to Tom. Their past didn't set their current relationship in stone. To empower Jeff, we discussed some simple guidelines to enable him to move into the role as listener in his relationships rather than fixer. I encouraged him to feel the discomfort of others' problems and sit with it; to show empathy. I shared with him the essence of this quote by Daniel Siegel:

> If our responses are intended to quickly fix a situation, we lose the opportunity to join with our children in a collaborative communication. Also, trying to fix our children's problems does not give respect to their own ability to think and figure out solutions to their own difficulties.[18]

I taught Jeff reflective listening, and that his job was to listen and not to try to solve. This was a novel and intimidating idea to him.

These practical assignments, though difficult for Jeff and Diane, encouraged them, because they had something within their power to work on while their son was away. Though they didn't fully grasp why they had to change their own behavior, they trusted the process enough to stick with it.

Significantly, these assignments also seized their attention and temporarily took their focus off Tom. This too was a relief, since Tom consumed most of their emotional energy. Jeff and Diane wrote to Tom that they were working with a counselor to focus on their own patterns. This allowed Tom more space for his own individuation process. As his parents wrote to Tom about their own therapeutic work, he in turn shared more freely about his experiences and insights. For the first time, Jeff, Diane and Tom were working side by side.

As the sessions progressed, Diane shifted emotionally. She admitted to feeling that she was coming out of darkness, as if she'd cleaned off a mirror, turned on the light, and had looked straight into it to see herself in full. "I realized how my whole life I have never really shared who I am. . . . I now see my tendency to avoid my emotions and the emotions of others. . . . I like to be alone and do my own thing; it is more comfortable. This work on emotional awareness in relationships and being present in the family is exhausting. Yet, I also see how in my efforts to avoid pain, I also avoid joy; I am uncomfortable with all emotions."

With this tremendous insight, Diane courageously stepped out of her comfort zone and developed awareness of her life-long pattern of emotional avoidance. The insight allowed her to have a new understanding of her son. She continued: "I find now, rather than blaming my son and myself for his addictions and failures, I can see that he is a lot like me. I don't have addictive tendencies, but I have my own ways of shutting out emotions and I have suffered for it. Tom was just trying to numb out. I get it now. Unfortunately, numbing out sucked him in and he was forced to get help; whereas I was just on autopilot."

To address Diane's "exhaustion," we discussed ways to set up personal boundaries and establish a balance between over-involvement in another's emotions and shutting off feelings altogether. For example, she could say to Jeff: "I want to hear how you're feeling, but I'm noticing how tired I am. Can you tell me more at breakfast?" In this communication, she would be bringing herself and an awareness of her emotions into the conversation, rather than just shutting off. I also encouraged Diane to integrate more self-care into her life, which might allow her to be more emotionally available for her family. This, too, was uncomfortable for Diane; but she identified that she liked going on walks and that needlepoint helped her relax. So she tried to be more conscious of doing one thing for herself each day. Despite her hesitancy, Diane admitted to feeling motivated by her new insight and awareness; yet she also felt unsure of how much real change she was capable of.

The critical thing to understand about this pattern of denial and avoidance is that kids in treatment undergo exactly the same thing. It's one thing to gain awareness of a problem; it's something else to change the behavior, break the habit, or transcend the addiction. Diane observed the tension of this distinction and in the process made a discovery similar to the one Tom likely did in his process. Parents can relate to their kids in this parallel way. Adolescents and young adults come to understand how they feel and discover why they're engaging in unhealthy behaviors and patterns. For them, too, the fog lifts, and they feel reinvigorated and self-aware.

Yet, most people are reluctant to change their behavior. Kids will still say, "I know I can go back to college now and control myself at parties," or "I know I can go back to my [abusive] boyfriend and our relationship will be so much better now, because I can communicate." There are still layers of denial. Yet, seeing this parallel process between your child and yourself can create room for compassion and a deeper level of understanding. Tense and anxious parents can soften and feel a deeper empathy for their children's struggles, by joining with them. When parents personally feel challenged when attempting to change their own habits and patterns, they can see their child's process in a new light. Change is hard.

Moreover, a parallel process exists when you stay with feelings of uncertainty, rather than reacting to them. Every day, Tom has to reconcile his own uneasy, uncertain thoughts and feelings about his future. Jeff and Diane could join with Tom in this process of being with uncomfortable emotions, rather than finding a shortcut to shut downs, exaggerations, or catastrophic thinking. This is the true process of empathy.

For his part, Jeff began to practice a new skill called "reflective listening." The core steps to reflective listing are as follows:

- **Be Present**—Begin by focusing on the person
- **Mirror/Validate**—Reflect what you're observing/hearing and validate the feelings
- **Allow the Child to Problem-solve**
- **Ask Questions**
- **Keep the Door Open**

These skills allow one to slow down, listen, ask questions, and be present with another. There is no "fixing" in reflective listening. In fact, I asked Jeff to refrain from giving an opinion, advice, or suggestion—to consciously take himself out of the conversation. So, when Brett came home after he'd had a fight with a friend at soccer practice, Jeff practiced:

Jeff: "Hey Brett, what's up? You look upset." (*Mirroring*)

Brett: "Oh, I'm just mad. Alex was pretty mean and aggressive at soccer. It's nothing."

Jeff: "I hear that you're mad and see that you're upset. It's tough when kids are mean." (*Reflecting, validating*)

Brett: "Yeah."

Jeff: "What do you think you're going to do about it?" (*Allowing Brett to problem-solve*)

Brett: "It's not that big of a deal. I'm just going to blow it off."

Jeff: "Well, let me know if you want to talk more." (*Keeping the door open*)

Brett: "Thanks Dad."

It was extremely hard for Jeff not to insert his ideas and opinions, yet he practiced listening, being patient, and doing nothing. He had to refrain in earnest, to resist making a suggestion or giving a solution. With time, he actually got into the assignment; and although it felt unnatural just to listen, he noticed that people were sharing more with him.

Meanwhile, bumps and obstacles were always coming up in Tom's treatment. Tom's setbacks seemed to also trigger relapses in the family:

Jeff's emotions would be amplified and so would his efforts to rescue, while Diane would freeze over emotionally and feel paralyzed. Yet, they continued to engage in weekly therapy sessions and, with time, began to see these obstacles and setbacks as opportunities to practice their new skills. It was recommended that Tom transition to a sober-living program after his wilderness experience. Tom went willingly, though he still unloaded onto his parents when he felt frustrated. On the first phone call, Tom said, "When can I go back to my college? You can't keep me away forever."

Recognizing that Tom was blaming others and not taking responsibility, Jeff was tempted to get defensive and lecture him, but he stopped himself:

> **Jeff**: "Sounds like you're feeling angry or frustrated at Mom and me." (*Mirroring, validating*)
>
> **Tom**: "No, I just don't like it here."
>
> **Jeff**: "Oh, that's hard. What is it like? Can you tell me more about it?" (*Validating, asking questions*)
>
> **Tom**: "Well, I guess it's okay. I just miss my wilderness group and also my college buds."
>
> **Jeff**: "Oh yeah, I can imagine that. How do the other kids cope with that?" (*Validating and encouraging Tom to problem-solve*)
>
> **Tom**: "Well, in three weeks we're able to write letters. I definitely want to write Ryan. I was mad at him, but I can see that he helped me out a lot."
>
> **Jeff**: "That sounds great. Thanks for telling us how you feel. We're working on listening and really want to be able to support you." (*Showing vulnerability*)

Another area of anxiety that persisted, despite Tom's and the parents' progress, was their deep, hidden fear that Tom might not make it. As their therapist, I had to expose this fear, since its undercurrents were too overpowering and destabilizing. Diane and Jeff revealed that a close friend of the family had lost their son to a meth addiction and the thought that Tom might go the same way chilled them. When I asked Diane and Jeff if they believed that Tom also had the potential to recover from his addictions, they struggled to answer.

Exposing this fear caused Jeff and Diane pain. When kids enter treatment, parents tend to view the child through the lens of his vulnerability and inability to navigate struggle and problems successfully. It felt important to emphasize a more holistic perspective of Tom, so I asked Jeff and Diane to highlight their son's strengths by identifying the times throughout his childhood when he'd made good choices, went against the grain, expressed vulnerability, showed thoughtfulness, persevered, succeeded, and triumphed. Although Tom's life and future were in his own hands, his parents had to uncover hope and faith in his strengths. Tom, too, needed to know that others saw his assets, even or especially when he couldn't.

Diane and Jeff chronicled their positive memories of Tom's life—the times of connection and success, and areas of reoccurring strength. They found this heartening. The exercise brought to light many forgotten, fond remembrances that had been trampled by pervasive feelings of worry and disconnection. Diane and Jeff weren't glossing over the difficulties, they were acknowledging that the moments when Tom had acted positively were also part of his story. They recalled Tom's closeness to and protectiveness of Brett; his thoughtful essays published in a journal; the free-spiritedness they readily witnessed on summer vacations to the beach; his love for animals and small children; and his volunteer efforts for the humane society. They acknowledged Tom's ease with computers and technology, how he was the IT person in the family. They commented on his natural athleticism and his successes in cross-country running; they honored his brilliance and intelligence and high test-scores; they relished his love of cooking; and lastly, they recognized that, despite the fact he acted out, Tom always made nice friends.

This was quite a list. I asked Diane and Jeff to think of these attributes when they spoke to Tom, to send the loving message that there was more to him than addictions, depression, and struggle. This seemed to help mitigate their overwhelming fear.

Though this act of reframing, Diane's new self-awareness and Jeff's new listening skills didn't directly fix or change anything with Tom; they nonetheless dramatically shifted Diane and Jeff's perspectives. Diane gained new insights about herself, compassion for Tom, and even gratitude for being able to grow during this difficult time. Jeff admitted to feeling useful, and saw the benefits of his new skill: "I actually feel like I'm getting something accomplished, even though I'm doing nothing. At least I have a strategy now." He finally let go of the idea that he had to fix Tom's problems, and was able to sleep better at night. They felt less despair and some renewed hope.

More importantly, they were able to practice their skills and work on their patterns every day, to the direct benefit of Brett and Jenna. Diane spent time sharing more with Jenna on the phone and attuning to Brett's emotions at home, which she felt deepened these relationships. Jeff stopped problem-solving and worked on learning from and listening to his children. Jeff and Diane were also able eventually to share more with each other. Having a child in treatment is an enormous burden on a marriage and it's difficult to manage it all in an emotionally healthy way. Once Jeff and Diane focused on their own processes, they were able to share with each other and gain from the other's heightened self-awareness, listening skills, and emotional attunement.

Tom's road to recovery will be long. But when Jeff and Diane flew out to his program for their first parent-visit, they felt more confident and at ease. Irrespective of Tom, Diane and Jeff had new skills they knew would help in rebuilding their relationship and trust. They were a little nervous, but both admitted that all they could control were their own responses, their ability to be open, and their ability to listen. They weren't so worried about how much "progress" Tom was making, because they realized that it was up to him: it was his life.

Because they were learning to let go, Jeff and Diane noticed that it was probably the best visit with Tom they'd ever had. They laughed, were open, enjoyed each other, and were less fearful. They knew how hard recovery was, often involving relapse, yet they felt they were on the right path and were more connected as a family. And at a core level, they felt deeply proud of the emotional work Tom was doing, because he'd helped spark change and self-discovery in them.

chapter 6

MEETING YOUR CHILD HALFWAY

SENDING YOUR CHILD to treatment, therapy, and for some, numerous programs can be enormously costly. Not only are the financial sacrifices many families make colossal, but the emotional expense and the amount of time and energy that parents give can be huge. To preserve the gains made by your adolescent or young adult, parents have to meet their child halfway, by doing their own work alongside their child as did Jeff and Diane. This chapter will more carefully examine the patterns that parents may have.

IDENTIFYING YOUR PATTERN

Everybody has their own way of reacting and responding to emotional issues and problems. When their daughter is raging and verbally abusive, or their son is shut down and refuses to go to school, each parent has their own way of navigating the emotional landscape of the home. What is most important is to know the way *you* do it. What's your pattern when you've passed your limit, when you feel in over your head, when the demands of the moment are exceeding your own internal resources? Below is a list of patterns I've observed in parents with troubled teens.

- **Rescuing**: doing whatever you can to take away your child's discomforts in attempt to make your child happy.
- **Yelling**: using guilt, blame, or threats to attempt to get your child to listen.
- **Withdrawing**: resorting to silence and isolating from your child or the conflict.
- **Finding distractions**: always looking for something else to focus on, planning future events, and keeping busy.
- **Stoicism**: removing yourself emotionally from any conflict and responding in a detached, unaffected way.
- **Workaholism**: finding ways to avoid the home and stay at work where you feel more effective and more in-control (or working in the home and avoiding family life).
- **Lecturing**: looking to explain, solve, fix the problem—telling your child what to do and what should be happening.
- **Addictions**: engaging excessively in whatever brings a feeling of escape: alcohol, computer and Internet abuse, gambling, etc.
- **Worrying**: constantly going to the worst-case scenario, perpetually feeling unrest, and fearing a catastrophe.

All of us are capable of falling into many of these patterns, not just one. Diane was withdrawn, stoic, and looked for distractions; Jeff rescued, lectured, and worried, and became an insomniac. These patterns shouldn't make parents feel guilty or blamed, but they must simply acknowledge what's probably happening in the home. Remember, the goal is self-awareness. If parents can identify one, two, or even three patterns they fall into, they will have taken a courageous first step toward solving them, because the reality is that everybody has work to do. Nobody responds to everything in an emotionally healthy and mature way, especially when dealing with a troubled teen. In order to break your pattern, you must own it, gain awareness of your underlying emotion, become accountable, and lastly intentionally respond in a new way. By cycling through these steps and developing these skills, parents can become role models for emotional maturity.

I cannot emphasize enough how difficult it can be to "own" one's stuff. The biggest hurdle for parents can be admitting they don't know everything and are imperfect. Knowing one's own weaknesses is one thing, but admitting them in the process of having a child in treatment can often elicit more distress, since many parents harbor feelings of failure. What is critical to distinguish is that parents don't need to own the whole problem, certainly not their child's choices, but instead look courageously at their own patterns.

HOW TO BREAK YOUR PATTERN

1) Self-knowledge

Some parents may be able to read the list above and their pattern or patterns may jump off the page at them. They know exactly what they do when they're overwhelmed or fearful. For other parents, it may not be as clear. We all have blind spots and it's much easier to see your husband, child, or mother's pattern than your own. However, no parent can be accountable for his or her pattern or know how to change it without developing self-knowledge.

Self-knowledge comes from seeing yourself clearly and accurately. Most people have a somewhat skewed self-image. Some may view themselves more positively, seeing their strengths and overlooking their weaknesses; others may view themselves more negatively, observing everything with a critical eye. In reality, we all have strengths and weaknesses; self-knowledge is looking honestly at them. However, because looking inward is so difficult, most people need the help of others to gain a fuller awareness of their habits and patterns.

Talking to a friend, therapist, or spouse is an excellent way to gain self-awareness. But it's critically important to feel safe emotionally in the relationship you have with the friend, therapist, or spouse, and know that he or she is giving you feedback compassionately and isn't trying to hurt you. Genuine feedback is a rare gift. Still, most people are reluctant to hear anything negative about their behaviors, actions, or character; yet it can be invaluable when someone provides you with a broader perspective that enhances your self-knowledge.

Feedback can also highlight strengths and positive attributes of which you may not have been aware. Employers often give employees both positive and constructive feedback about their performance and this allows professionals to grow and gain more confidence in their skills. Likewise, feedback in a family provides an important opportunity to grow, develop awareness, and gain confidence in your relationships. Asking a friend, therapist, or spouse what they see your patterns to be is a courageous step toward deepening your self-knowledge.

If it feels safe, parents can even ask their child for feedback or their perspective. Kids have intimate knowledge of their parents, and both are deeply vulnerable to the other. Yet parents (and kids) put immense energy into protecting themselves. Parents put on their own armor and justify their actions, which only reinforces the parent–child divide. If parents want to break through to their children, they can soften or dissolve their defenses, and join with their struggling kids in becoming more self-aware. To do this, parents need to place more value on joining in than on protection.

2) Self-attunement

As I've argued throughout this book, attunement to others is an essential quality in relationships. However, before we can read others' emotions, we first need to develop the capacity to attune internally to our own emotions and feelings, exemplified by Diane with her "feelings journal." As Daniel Siegel writes: "Emotional relating requires a mindful awareness of our own internal state as well as being open to understanding and respecting our child's state of mind."[19]

When we're aware of our underlying emotions—fear, sadness, powerlessness, and so on—we become more cognizant of what is driving our actions and habits. For example, if a mother realizes that she tends to yell reactively at her kids when she's overwhelmed, then attuning is taking the opportunity to understand what she's feeling internally. Perhaps she's feeling pressure at work, or is tense about a fight she had the previous night with her daughter, which they never resolved. Perhaps she's worried because her son is failing math. Whatever it may be, the lack of awareness of her underlying emotions is causing this mother to play out her pattern (yelling) rather than staying with the underlying emotion.

Before parents can break patterns, it's crucial they attune to these underlying emotions and feelings. Once they do this, parents can communicate their feelings and kids can develop empathy for their parents; identifying and managing emotions is on-going for children and adults alike.

You can attune to your emotions in many ways, and it's best for individuals to identify what method works best for them. In wilderness programs, the group conducts a "feelings check" roughly three times a day. Each person in the group stops and identifies what they're feeling in the moment—a process that for kids is initially like learning a new language. I have frequently handed out "feelings sheets" and the students simply had to identify the word that best described how they were feeling. This daily practice becomes routine—and, with this, adolescents become adept at identifying their emotions. In a feelings check, the focus is not to share thoughts (which is easy to do), but merely to identify the feeling *words*.

For example, it's easy to say, "I didn't feel like getting up today; it was cold out and I miss my bed at home. But I'm okay." In this statement, little information is given about the internal emotional landscape. Instead, we ask kids to label the feeling words: "I felt *homesick* when I woke up, and now I feel *engaged* and *present*." This powerful practice gives specific information about emotions and is essential to effective communication. When kids identify their feelings, they own their internal experience; they aren't blaming or escaping. When a boy says, "I feel sad when I think of my mom," nobody can tell this teen that his feeling is right or wrong. When adolescents communicate what's true for them, others can grasp and understand their internal experience. This is often a teen's first step in feeling seen and heard.

For parents who aren't doing "feelings checks" experientially in a group process three times a day, other means exist. As described in the previous chapter, "feelings journals" are great avenues for attunement. These aren't journals to vent and blame others, they're purely meant to identify feelings and emotions throughout the day. Talking with a loved one or therapist is also an effective way to identify and communicate feelings. Even meditation can be a profound vehicle for attunement: one takes an opportunity to sit, breathe, be still, and be present. Part of being present is attuning to whatever's going on: whether it's tension in your shoulder, sadness that your child is struggling, frustration with the phone company, gratitude that your father's health is improving, worry about the future. If we attune to feelings, we give them each a place. We're allowing them to be there. We're not acting out a pattern as a means for escape.

An essential component of attunement is learning to sit with your emotions, however painful they may be. Our culture favors avoiding or escaping unwanted feelings; learning to identify and be with them is a life-skill. In the wilderness, the avenues a teenager may take to escape their habits and patterns aren't available: they can't consume junk food, drugs, or alcohol; they can't switch on the TV or computer; they can't gossip on their cell phones, isolate themselves in their room, and so on. In the desert, they're forced to stay with their feelings and encouraged to talk about them.

In this process, counselors and group members don't attempt to cheer the kids up or make it better. Instead, they honor what each individual is going through:

- "I feel so guilty I lied to my parents."
- "I miss my girlfriend and I worry that she's not okay."
- "I'm so mad at myself for failing out of school."

- "I'm really scared I'm going to relapse when I go home."
- "I'm still angry that my dad sold my car."

These are examples of powerful feelings that kids express; they feel validated and heard when these feelings are each given a place.

In the treatment process, kids learn that when they sit with feelings and honor them, those feelings fade—even anger, anxiety, guilt, and sadness. Life is constantly moving; unpleasant and pleasant things are always happening. If we allow ourselves to feel uncomfortable emotions, and not react to them, those feelings can pass, instead of acting out patterns as a means for escape and digging a deeper hole for ourselves. For example, a mother may think, "I not only feel overwhelmed about work, but now I also feel guilty for yelling at my kids." Or a child may think, "Now I have low-self esteem and an addiction. Before, I just felt bad about myself; now I am really a f—— up." With self-knowledge and self-attunement, we have the choice to break our patterns and not take the unhealthy avenues for escaping and avoiding our feelings.

3) Accountability
The next step in breaking your pattern is to accept accountability for it. When parents do this it can shift the whole dynamic in a parent–child relationship. Parents need to own their patterns not only for their own growth, but also as a means of halting their child's constant onslaughts.

Through the years of working with adolescents and young adults, I've seen that kids are much more focused on their parents' behavior than their own; likewise, parents are much more focused on their kids' patterns and behavior than their own. Children are not only expert projectors—"If I can focus on Mom's yelling then I can keep the heat on her"—but teens use their parents' behavior as an excuse or justification for their own problems. It's easier to find faults in, or focus on, others—anything to circumvent looking internally.

To have genuine behavioral change, parents need to cycle through these steps so frequently that they become new healthy patterns: self-knowledge, attunement, accountability, and intentional responses. Through reinforcing this process you can short-circuit reactive habits and replace them with productive ones. I'll give two examples.

RITA AND PAM

Rita was fourteen and loved to put her mother, Pam, down. She was ruthless, describing her mother as dramatic, controlling, and mean. "My mother is crazy," she said. "All she does is worry and try to control me. It's really too much. I mean when she walks the dog around the block, she has to put the house alarm on because she thinks I'm going to run away. I feel like I'm in a jail cell. She yells really mean things at me; she even called me 'a slut.' She hates my friends. She always criticizes how I dress. It's like she wants me to dress so preppy. But then at other times, she buys me these really skimpy things and doesn't let me wear them." Rita went on and on. She found it entertaining to ridicule her mother, while at the same time keeping the focus off her.

In treatment, the focus was on Rita. Her parents, though recently divorced, had volatile fights and ongoing tensions, which spilled over onto Rita and her brother. Though she described the divorce as a godsend, Rita was overwhelmed by grief regarding the ensuing loss of security and stability of her family. In my work with Rita, I first drew a boundary. I told Rita that before we could talk about her mother's behavior, she first needed to disclose how she treated Pam. Initially, Rita laughed, but then became antsy. When I held firm and refused to let her divert her attention to her mother, Rita dropped her head and could barely look up at me. She felt ashamed. Before my eyes, she instantly transitioned from deflecting all emotions to becoming apparently flooded with guilt. Tearfully, she admitted her harsh and cruel behavior. After a long pause, Rita pulled herself together and shared some examples. Some of what she revealed I already knew from her mother, but was encouraged to hear Rita's accounts: "Did she tell you how I stole clothes out of her closet that she just bought, which still had the tags on; that are, like, really expensive clothes? One dress I ruined. I also stole her jewelry, stuff that she didn't wear, or at least that's how I justified it."

Rita had been sneaking out with an older boy named Brian, with whom she'd become sexually involved. Brian had already been arrested for shoplifting, so Pam refused to let Rita see him. "I gave the jewelry to my boyfriend to sell," continued Rita. "I am terrible. I even forced my younger brother to lie for me. I told him that I'd never play with him again if he told Mom that I was at Brian's house, when I was supposed to be at Karen's house."

Rita continued: "I guess I took my anger out on her. I say terrible, mean things, like I hate her; I even called her 'a bitch.'" Rita began to sob. She'd become so deep in her lies, projecting all her faults onto her mother, that she'd lost sight of her own behavior. Admission of guilt is a positive first step, because it forced Rita to begin to talk about herself and her own actions.

Rita needed to process her emotions and begin to become accountable for her behavior. What helped was that Pam also began to become accountable. She, too, felt swamped by guilt, and at the insistence of her own therapist wrote to Rita. She admitted that she regretted yelling and calling her daughter names, and displacing onto Rita her anger at her ex-husband. Pam had been shocked to discover that her own daughter could engage in such vicious behavior, yet Pam had been acting out herself. Pam told me that because her trust level was so low, due to Rita's chronic lying, she needed to keep her daughter on a short leash. Still, she wished that she'd been more loving and had communicated in a more respectful way. She hoped in the future to listen more and understand Rita's feelings, before she made such harsh judgments. Pam felt terrible that they weren't closer, that they both treated each other with disdain. She knew that divorce was disrupting for everyone: she wished they could turn toward rather than away from each other, so they could get through this difficult time together.

When Rita received the letter, she immediately felt warmly toward her mother. Previously, she'd only talked about her mother in a sarcastic and demeaning manner. The letter prompted Rita to reach out to her mother. "Mom, I understand why you were so controlling, and mad," Rita wrote. "But I was the monster of the house, not you." For the first time, Rita and her mother began to talk openly, honestly, accountably, and with mutual respect.

When Pam owned her own behavior and cleaned up her side of the relationship, Rita couldn't hold it against her anymore and use it to justify her own acting out. She was forced to examine her own attitude, thoughts, and emotions. Rita came to understand her underlying fear and sadness that were the source of her behaviors. In the same manner, through her own therapeutic process, Pam began to feel optimistic, proud, and self-directed. Owning her patterns enabled her to see her situation more clearly, which gave her a sense of empowerment and healing. She also identified her regrets and thus created a place for new growth.

MICHAEL, LINDA, AND MAX

Michael was sixteen, an only child, who had severe problems motivating himself and suffered from depression and anxiety. He was overweight and his parents watched him sink deeper and deeper into his own apathy, which resulted in more inactivity, more weight gain, and more depression. Michael was very bright, yet his intelligence seemed to further disable him. He refused to go to school and stayed in bed most of the day. However, he'd still read the *New York Times* from front to back. He was well-informed about world events and stated his opinions at home, yet in his own life he stayed safely away from any real-world situations. He felt school was boring. He was anxious socially, and gravely feared peer rejection. He avoided the whole teen world at all costs. Michael's parents became his best friends and only real relationships.

Michael's parents, Linda and Max, were deeply distraught and didn't know what to do. They had abundant empathy and compassion for Michael, but this seemed only to enhance their roles as enablers and their susceptibility to his manipulations. Michael could persuade them to doing everything for him, and they did because they felt terrible about his depression and being overweight.

Michael was sent to a wilderness-therapy program because Linda and Max knew something had to change. Surprisingly, Michael agreed to go willingly; however, this too backfired. Because he *chose* treatment, he thought that he could also "un-choose" it. After four days of struggle, he missed his bed and decided wilderness wasn't for him. Michael became extremely uncomfortable when he couldn't control the situation and didn't have his parents at his whim. The wilderness staff held him to the same standards that every wilderness student faced. For Michael, who believed that not all rules applied to him, it was a rude awakening.

Although Michael refused to start family therapy when he was home, Linda and Max did—they needed support. Though they developed some awareness of their parental roles, it still took time for them fully to see their patterns of enabling Michael. Max had a history of depression and alcohol abuse himself, and around the time Michael stopped going to school, roughly three months prior to his admission to the wilderness program, Max became deeply depressed. He took temporary leave from his job to care for Michael, while also resuming his own treatment with his psychiatrist. Linda was the stable figure. She was vice-president of a company and was adept at managing her own emotions and continuing to function, despite the turmoil in the family.

After weeks of despair, Michael realized that his parents were committed to him finishing the treatment program. Reluctantly, he started engaging in it, and it became evident that the exercise, fresh air, healthy meals, and lack of a couch or bed in which to hide were helping him. He made friends, talked about his depression and anxiety, and started to feel more energy and internal motivation. He discussed many subjects in therapy; yet one place he continued to get stuck was his entangled relationship with his dad. "It's my fault my dad is depressed," he said. "I caused it because I'm such a mess-up. I feel so terrible. I'm afraid he might go back to drinking. Krissy, I need to go home to help my dad. If I become a 'good' son, then maybe he won't be so depressed."

In this case, I had to urge Linda, Max, and Michael to start taking ownership for their patterns. "First off," I said to Michael, "if you're responsible for your dad's depression, then you must also be responsible for your mom's stability." He looked at me like I was crazy. "No, my mom is fine," he rebutted. "She's strong, and that's her [issue]."

"Well, isn't your dad's depression also his?" I replied. "From what I understand, he's had issues with depression that predate you having problems." This was startling to Michael. He felt so guilty about his dad's problems, and was sure his depression was his fault. Upon closer examination, it made sense why he felt this way. Michael was so worried about his dad and fixing his depression by being "good" and "nice," that he was effectively avoiding his own depression, low self-esteem, social anxiety, lack of motivation, apathy, and refusal to go to school.

In this process, Michael's parents were asked to take accountability for their "stuff." Max admitted in a letter to his long struggle with depression. The emotional turmoil in the home had affected him, though Max felt his depression stemmed more from stressors related to his job as a journalist and his own biochemistry. During the current episode, he'd returned to taking medication for depression and had refrained from using alcohol. He reported that he was feeling better and was back at work part-time. He also felt relief that Michael was getting help.

Linda identified her pattern of rescuing and avoiding conflict, which stemmed from her belief that her job was to hold everything together. She did help instill stability in the home, yet she also knew she went too far and did too much for Michael. Even with Michael's depression, she could have asked him to do small things around the house, to become responsible for some chores, some school involvement, and some amount of physical activity. "I felt so worried about your depression, your mental health," she wrote to her son, "that I was always rescuing you to try to make you feel better. I was afraid to ask you to do anything. I also feared your anger and backlash so much that I just acquiesced to all your demands. I am working on sitting with my anxiety and not reacting and rescuing. I need to become firmer in setting boundaries and being more accepting if you get mad at me."

As he read the letter, Michael felt anger fill his body; he'd assumed his parents would always provide comfort. Initially, he lashed out at his mother, through an angry letter. Yet, Linda stayed firm, and through the course of his wilderness experience, Michael came to see that his parents were right. His dad's depression was his; his mother had enabled him too much; and he had his own work to focus on. "My mom is right," he revealed in a letter to me. "I do need more boundaries. I had no motivation at home and I felt terrible doing nothing. Here I have to take care of myself, and my gear, and I do feel happier. I still struggle with a sense of doom, but it was not right to blame and manipulate my mom. I'm getting better at coping with my depression and talking to my group helps a lot. My new friends rock."

Owning patterns is essential for parents and adolescents to clear up resentments and regrets from the past, and move into the present. Accountability takes away issues of blame and allows each person to work toward more open dialogue.

4) Responding in a New Way

The last step in breaking patterns is to respond in a new way. There are multiple skills that fall under this heading, and these will be addressed in the coming chapters.

A BREATH OF FRESH AIR

When parents meet their kids halfway, they're bringing some fresh air into the relationship. Troubled teens and young adults are so accustomed to negative feedback—whether from parents, teachers, coaches, bosses, peers, or their own self-judgment and shame. Because many of these adolescents are used to messing up and causing problems, the labels and diagnoses stack up and damage their self-esteem and self-image. Whether parents express their disappointments to their child overtly or not, many teens and young adults in treatment feel like failures. They also feel their parents' eyes on their every step.

Adolescents need to discover their own thoughts, beliefs, and feelings. This process necessitates the safety of a container outside the constant supervision of mom and dad. Parents with a struggling teen walk the tightrope between providing more supervision for their child who's lying, defiant, and engaging in unhealthy behavior, and attempting to give their child the necessary space to individuate. Yet this is challenging to do in the home when all trust is broken. When parents know their child is away and safe in treatment, it's important for them to use not only the physical space but the corresponding emotional space to struggle and solve their own problems. When parents engage in their own process, and look inward they are giving their child this breathing room, they're meeting their child halfway.

chapter 7

LETTING GO OF THE REINS

ONCE PARENTS HAVE placed their child in treatment, all parents can do is engage in their own emotional work and employ the concepts of balanced parenting. They must recognize they cannot hold everything together, control their child's choices, or make their child happy. They cannot give their child sobriety, take away their child's depression, or give their child friends. They cannot ensure their child reaches his or her full potential. Invariably, when parents cling to this notion of making things better, the natural maturation process and individuation are impeded. At some point, parents have to let go. When they do, it's often a turning point.

MARTHA AND BOB

Martha and Bob were highly successful professionals. Martha was a primary-care physician and Bob the vice-president of a large media company. They knew how to thrive in many different contexts: they could manage difficult clients, treat complex patients, give lectures, preside on boards, travel the world, and gain the respect of others. Education was the chief focus for their two daughters, Olivia and Sophie, and performance at school was stressed above everything. Olivia was at a top-ranked college. Though she'd had her episodes of defiance and had been caught intoxicated multiple times, she demonstrated academic diligence and seemed to manage opposing stressors with ease.

Sophie, her seventeen-year-old younger sister, was artistically inclined, more anxious, less driven to achieve, and overall expressed a quiet, emotional sensitivity. She saw her sister as perfect and felt she could never please her parents in the same way. Whether she was clashing with Olivia or feeling inconsequential among her aggressive and petty peers, inadequate in math and science, or trivial in the eyes of her parents, Sophie felt hopeless and unable to manage these pressures. She loved art, film, dance, and music. Yet her parents saw this as fluff and not something to genuinely pursue. Sophie believed they didn't validate her as they did Olivia, who'd chosen to study medicine.

Sophie began to hang out with a small, seemingly "deviant" art crowd, which produced significant anxiety for Martha and Bob. Sophie continued to escalate her behavior to get her parents' attention. It was as if she felt: "If I can't fit the mold, I'm going to shake things up." And she did. Sophie experimented with heavy drugs, became sexually active, and, most problematically, became deeply involved in a volatile relationship with a troubled older boy named Jonah.

Martha and Bob weren't privy to how far Sophie had fallen or the degree of her emotional desperation. They did know, however, that Jonah was toxic. Sophie was codependent with him: she attempted to rescue him from drugs, assist him financially, and sort out his family problems. She gave him all her money, skipped school to be with him, and sneaked out to spend nights with him. She grew thin, wore ratty clothes, and barely bathed. Her whole life's focus became Jonah and their love. Yet, the pair had vicious fights—he even hit her once—though these conflicts seemed only to fuel intense make-up sessions. In the process, Sophie lost sight of herself, her needs, and her wants. She even relinquished her interests in art and film.

During this time, Sophie also scarcely acknowledged her parents. She treated the house both like a pit stop and a barrier to her being with Jonah all the time. Yet, since her mom and dad had lost emotional attunement and a connection with Sophie, they had no leverage—no way to tether her to the family unit. Whenever they implied anything negative about Jonah, Sophie went into a tailspin and quickly turned the tables. Her parents hated everything about her, she'd complain: her boyfriend, friends, art, and her clothes. Martha and Bob were unable to get through to her; still, they knew she was sinking fast.

Sophie was first sent off to a wilderness program and, subsequently, to an all-girl emotional-growth boarding school. Despite her initial kicking and screaming, and her deep sadness about leaving Jonah, Sophie did settle into her new world and embarked on the process of looking inward. Although she felt the rules were petty, Sophie also felt that her program *listened* to her and *saw* her. With time, she admitted to feeling happier, even more stable.

Martha and Bob, too, felt relief. Yet they soon realized how agonizing it was to have their daughter in the hands of others. Martha knew Sophie was safe, yet she worried incessantly about how she was doing: Was she sleeping? Was she eating? Was she making friends? What was her day like? Martha harbored catastrophic thoughts about the future. Meanwhile, Bob unloaded all cylinders the instant anything felt askew about the school. He relentlessly saw all the weaknesses in the program and wanted to give the organizers a lesson on how to run a business. He felt Sophie's advisor was inadequate and was only harming her educational future. Sophie was more intelligent than her peers, he would mention frequently, and she wasn't being challenged enough. He didn't understand all the emphasis on feelings. "I don't wake up and see if I *feel* like going to work," he argued. "I simply get up and go to work. This is what Sophie needs to understand." Bob was imposing, full of pride, and becoming more aggressive.

Martha, too, was bothered by the program. She couldn't understand why there were so many rules and boundaries. She and Bob were only allowed one chaperoned phone call a week, and Sophie was obliged to be on the program for at least six months before she could visit home. However, it was usually eight or nine months until students earned this privilege. Martha felt that, through the rules, the school was implying that she was an inadequate parent, although if she'd been honest with herself she'd have recognized that what she couldn't believe most was her loss of control as a mother. Martha missed Sophie a great deal and felt despair that they'd reached this point in their relationship.

In short, Bob and Martha were operating in their predicable patterns. Bob only felt comfortable when he saw aspects of Sophie to which he could relate, which lately had been nothing. He loved her: he tried to be open, but mostly acted like an attack dog. Martha was so anxious that she even started to blame the program for Sophie's struggles. In short, Martha and Bob were still trying to direct Sophie's life and missing the opportunity to attune to, and see the essence of, who she was.

This was highlighted by the alarm they felt when Sophie's counselors reported that she was painting daily, was interested in producing a short film, and hung out with the other artsy kids. Even as Martha and Bob could see that Sophie was making progress, responding to treatment and engaging in her own work, they were still mostly obstructed by their own grievances and disappointments.

For her part, Sophie could tell by Martha and Bob's frequent questions about academics, their silences when she brought up art, and their outright annoyance at the school boundaries, that they were still the same. With her own increased self-awareness, Sophie still felt awkward sharing her discoveries with her mom and dad. *They seemed too threatened by her progress.* At one point, Martha and Bob wanted to pull her out of the program and place her in a more academic prep school. Yet all the professionals signaled that this would disrupt Sophie's emotional work. She was, these experts said, building the internal resources necessary to navigate academic and social life; moving to such a school would just expose Sophie to these stressors again without the sufficient tools to handle them. Her parents were unconvinced, and even considered bringing her home. Yet they feared that Sophie would reconnect with Jonah, who had become the enemy.

LETTING GO OF THE REINS: WITH THE TREATMENT PROCESS

Many adolescents and young adults who engage in reckless behavior are attempting to communicate through their behavior. They don't know how to talk about their problems, so they largely act them out. Our task, as parents and counselors, is to make sure we're listening and decoding the communication properly. When parents are unable to decode, repair, and set their child on the right path again, adolescent therapists and treatment programs with skilled professionals can help their child resume their emotional development. At this point, parents need to let go of the reins.

Of course, feedback is important. However, it is critical to distinguish whether you're faulting the school because you feel powerless or you're giving genuine feedback. Bob and Martha were hindering treatment because the program staff had to put copious amounts of energy into them to put them "at ease," which resulted in the focus being taken off Sophie. They were failing to look inward and address their own anxiety.

In some cases, parents also directly undermine the program by promising their child a vacation when she's finished with the program or a shopping spree if she works hard. These arrangements are problematic because they continue the pattern of the parent making deals with the child for outcomes desired by the parent, rather than allowing the child to discover the reward of feeling pride in accomplishing a self-defined goal. Do parents really want the program to fulfill their agenda, or help their daughter become an emotionally mature and resilient individual? When parents again engage their teen as if she's a small child—jumping in to meet her demands, trying to direct her life, or attempting to make everything better—they're denying her any responsibility or emotional maturity and may reverse many gains made by the treatment.

LETTING GO OF THE REINS: WITH YOUR CHILD

Parents need to let go of their own strong opinions of their child, and allow the latter to figure out and develop their own beliefs, thoughts, feelings, interests, goals, and pursuits. Kids know what their parents want: for them to go to school, to make good choices, to uncover their potential. Yet if they lack internal resources and internal navigation, then adolescents will either adopt their parents' beliefs or rebel against them. Regrettably, doing the latter too frequently results in the child abusing substances, skipping or refusing to go to school, lying, shutting down, being defiant, and so on. However, because parents loom large in the eyes of an undifferentiated young person with poor confidence and esteem, adopting mom and dad's viewpoints can be equally problematic—if they only do so to please their parents, rather than making choices that resonate with their own true nature.

The treatment process often allows kids to come to know what they want, believe, think, and feel. However, kids are often reluctant to share these realizations because they're so susceptible to what they perceive as the unwavering opinions of their parents. If a son admits to being an addict, for instance, he may fear that it will either confirm what his parents think or upset them. Instead, this young man's emerging individuation must be validated and reflected. Parents don't need to weigh in; it's his process. Rather than having an opinion, parents can say: "Sounds like you're making some important discoveries."

But the result may well be to the parents' satisfaction anyway: many kids come to realize that they *want* to graduate college, quit drugs, pursue their own interests, and clean up their list of regrets.

Still, they need to *own* their future steps as their own desires, not fulfill what their parents want.

Sophie realized she was different from her family, and that she needed to explore her thoughts and feelings away from the set beliefs of her family. She admitted that she'd always felt deeply spiritual, yet no one in her family believed in God. She knew she excelled in the arts, was sensitive, emotional, loved animals and nature, and didn't have a competitive bone in her body. These were all her conclusions. Her insight into her past behaviors and her awareness of her emotions grew; yet it took time to share these emerging beliefs and insights with her parents.

Another critical area that parents need to let go is in their belief that school is the priority. Parents with children in treatment often fail to comprehend that as bright and promising as their child may be, their emotional problems are making it impossible for them to utilize their full intelligence. These young people are being crippled by their all-consuming emotions. I've found from working with troubled teens that they don't have the energy for academic pursuits; it's all allocated to their emotional tumult. Only when the emotional frenzy has been doused will rationality reemerge. This takes time. In my experience with wilderness programs, it takes a while for kids to reset. After perhaps a month or more of "I feel" statements, sleeping and eating regularly, subsisting without addictions and unhealthy habits, and another month of self-reflection in individual and group therapy, kids begin to awaken to the present moment, where they're not caught up in maintaining a false image or reacting to external stimulation. The thirst to learn and engage their intellect reappears; children find they want to think things through rather than always to react to them.

Sophie's emotional angst needed to be addressed first before her academics could become the priority. Only when she was aware of her internal process, was managing her range of feelings, and feeling a degree of self-control, could she resume her education. This is the primary process—coming to know one's own thoughts and feelings through healthy individuation while addressing one's emotional deficiencies. Only through this process could Sophie free herself to be available for learning.

LETTING GO OF THE REINS:
MOM AND DAD'S SELF-PROTECTION

Many kids with primary problems—such as poor emotional management, lack of resiliency, and limited self-discipline—often compensate through relying on other areas of strength. They may excel in a school subject, at sport, in the arts, or in the pursuit of a personal hobby. These exploits can build esteem, strengthen the ego, and foster internal resolve. For example, a boy with ADHD and dyslexia may struggle socially and emotionally, but as the star soccer player he may still be equipped with the necessary internal resources. He may still be in difficulty, though not to the degree that all areas of his life are unraveling or where he needs to be removed from the home. Unfortunately, many kids who enter treatment have no successes or positive outlets to lean on. Sophie, without either internal resources or artistic pursuits substantiated and encouraged by her parents, had nothing to sustain her, no wherewithal to navigate high school.

The secondary, parallel process was repairing Bob and Martha's dynamic with their child. It was up to Sophie to gain resilience for her vulnerability and emotional sensitivity. Yet Bob and Martha had exacerbated the problem through their heavy-handed approach to parenting, their lack of attunement and validation, and their inability to see their younger daughter in full. Bob and Martha had to address their own inability to see, acknowledge, and validate Sophie.

Through months of anguish and at the insistence of Sophie's therapist, Martha and Bob eventually began to let go and started their own therapy. Although they'd initially gone begrudgingly, Martha and Bob found therapy useful and productive. At a minimum, it provided them with an outlet to share their frustrations, which their skilled, empathic therapist was able to reframe through identifying tasks involving listening and letting go for each parent.

Bob admitted he was aggressive, emotionally blinded, and had been unable to validate Sophie. Martha acknowledged that her own feeling of failure had caused her to shut down and had prevented her from intervening appropriately. That feeling of failure had further resulted in her hostility toward the program. Bob had patterns of yelling, lecturing, and workaholism; Martha withdrew, found distractions, and worried. As they began to look at these forms of emotional escape with their therapist, Bob and Martha saw that, like Sophie, they had their own work cut out for them. They became more compassionate toward Sophie as they realized that neither of them had been emotionally available to her, and they began to understand why she relied so heavily on Jonah.

Sophie noticed changes in her parents, and began to share more openly. She told them of how painful emotionally it had been to grow up in such a high-achieving family. She told them how hurt she'd been when her art was unacknowledged and that she felt overwhelmed because she didn't know how to manage all the pressures of high school. She said she felt sadness and shame for being mean to her sister. She also expressed penetrating insight into why she clung to Jonah, and why he became her world. He saw her, and understood her and her art, she related, even though she knew he was using her. But she acknowledged that she was also using him—as an outlet for her rebellion, and her way to communicate that all wasn't okay. With this insight, she also saw her vulnerable place she put herself in. She had risked a lot for Jonah, and it scared her to think that this might happen again.

Sophie began to share, and her parents began to listen. They stepped away and let her be in charge; they let *her* explain who she was, what she was feeling, and what she needed. In other words, they *attuned.* As if for the first time, they saw her for who she was instead of projecting onto her what they wanted her to be and highlighting her inadequacies. In other words, they *validated* her. They made amends; they expressed their gratitude.

As Bob and Martha stepped back, Sophie stepped forth with a stronger sense of self. Martha and Bob admitted that they'd rediscovered not only their daughter, but themselves as well. Attuning to their own emotions each day, they reported, enabled them to feel more alive, more present. Even when they felt uneasy, fearful, and powerless, at least they were aware of these emotions rather than being emotionally asleep. Bob and Martha tried as best as they could to stay with these uncomfortable feelings, rather than resume their old patterns. It was a process of trial and error, at once daunting and awakening.

There is freedom in letting go. Though they did so reluctantly, Bob and Martha not only released their younger daughter, but they let go of their projections and their shortsightedness. By looking inward, they relinquished the reins to Sophie, while also gaining their own fresh perspective. They exposed their vulnerabilities, flaws, and dysfunctional habits. In their therapy, they discovered that they provided a lot of structure and boundaries for Sophie, but they missed attuning to who she was, and it was critical to right this imbalance. They wrote to Sophie and began to take accountability; the warmth and connection brought Sophie to tears.

In the process, Martha and Bob discovered a daughter with emotional depth, artistic aptitude, and an acute perceptiveness to emotional subtleties in others. They saw Sophie anew. Getting to know Sophie again took them out of their protective shells, and in the process they grew, and felt more freedom and openness toward themselves and others, to both pain and joy. They let go of blame. Though Martha and Bob knew they had strong habits of shutting down feelings and that developing self-awareness was a lifelong process, they also knew it was a worthwhile endeavor because it brought them closer to Sophie and allowed them to really see and know her. With this, Sophie got better.

In hindsight, Martha and Bob felt that Sophie's path, though torturous, had taken the whole family to a new place of openness and connection they'd never had before: she had steered the way. Rather than feeling like the underachiever of the family, Sophie became the catalyst for change. Rather like a twisted wheel needs to be taken off the bike and given adequate reinforcements so that it can be true, Sophie had needed to be taken out of her family and placed in the hands of others so that she could ride more easily through the journey of life. Sophie fine-tuned her problem-solving skills, and gained resourcefulness and inner strength. Martha and Bob had needed to be stranded to wake up to their own denial.

Sophie pulled her grades together and was accepted at a top art school; she had incredible talent. Martha and Bob fully let go. They saw Sophie was a skilled individual, though not in the same manner to which they were accustomed. They felt proud to see her excel in an area in which they were novices. They learned from her, and furthermore, felt humbled by both her emotional strength and the sensitivity that came out in her art.

Parents *must* let go. Moreover, they ought to switch the focus to themselves and begin to work on what they *can* control, such as self-awareness. When parents genuinely support the treatment process and stop looking to place blame outside their child, it makes a difference. When parents let their son struggle in the program, their daughter learns to problem-solve, and the clinicians respond in the way they see fit, and then get on board with their own emotional work, truly the ship will sail in the direction that everyone wants.

chapter 8

THE ART OF REFRAMING

Shifting Responsibility Back to Your Child

A COMMON FEATURE of many families with an adolescent or young adult in treatment is that the parent and child only relate in a narrow, confined way. The child expresses a need or problem and a parent works to meet the need or solve the problem. Kids are reduced to talking to their parents only if they want something or if something is wrong. This has become the primary, and for some, the only avenue of communication between parent and child.

If your child has started a therapeutic program, you may have seen new dynamics emerge. Your child may be expressing more thoughts and feelings. He may have disclosed more about his behavior and his choices at home; or she may have revealed more of her inner world. In essence, your child has started the process of *sharing*, which is a wonderful new way to communicate, to feel emotionally close. Moreover, it allows parents to have a much broader understanding of how their child experiences the world.

Still, there will be occasions, perhaps many of them, when the age-old pattern of kids looking to parents to meet their needs, solve their problems, and rescue them from a hardship will reemerge. This resurfacing touches a nerve and discourages parents, prompting them to feel as though no progress has been made, as though they're back to where they started. For others, it can be a subtle, familiar, and easy way to reengage an old pattern. In either case, parents don't know how to respond differently. They feel guilty if they don't help their child, yet they also feel embarrassed or inadequate if they fall back into the rut of rescuing and fixing problems.

An alternative way to respond exists: *reframing*. When a child frames an issue or problem as a parent's responsibility, the task for parents who want their child to solve their own problems and mature emotionally is to reframe who's responsible for the problem.

MEGAN AND HER PARENTS

Megan was fifteen when she was enrolled in a wilderness-therapy program. She was an only child; developmentally, she struggled verbally with speech and communication, which affected her social skills. She was affectionate with her parents, yet was never a talker or sharer. She had a small frame, was always a picky eater, and barely spoke at meals. She would only take a few bites and then ask to be excused. Megan preferred TV and computer games and spent a lot of time alone in her room.

Megan's parents were affluent and had indulged her materialistically since she was a small child. Desperate to connect and show affection, Megan's parents frequently took her shopping and it became the preferred way to relate—specifically, her father loved to "spoil" her. When shopping, Megan was more verbal; she'd say what she did and didn't like. She became versed in the world of fashion and was good at telling her parents what she needed and wanted. With this, Megan felt she could express herself.

Because she struggled socially, Megan fast-forwarded into physical relationships with boys. Although there was little talking, Megan felt like she was connecting with guys; she felt close. As her emphasis on fashion grew, Megan wanted more "designer clothes," and it became evident that her clothes were maturing faster than she was. Her cyber-world grew as well, and she put more and more explicit content on her MySpace page. Eventually, when inappropriate and sexually pro-vocative pictures of her were circulated around the school, Megan was asked to leave her school. She refused to talk about what had happened, and, not surprisingly, her parents were devastated. Knowing that talk therapy had never been effective with Megan and that she couldn't return to her school, her parents chose the experiential approach of a wilderness-therapy program. They also hoped to get a clinical assess-ment of what Megan needed in a new school.

Megan kept to herself initially in the program. She rarely spoke, only uttering a few complaints and some requests for special food. At the same time, Megan's parents' anxiety multiplied with her out of the home and being unable to care for her. They worried that she would get "so dirty," and knowing she was a picky eater they grew con-cerned about what she was eating. They also feared she wasn't "rugged" enough for wilderness. In treatment, however, it became increasingly clear that Megan needed to grow emotionally. She needed skills for communication, sharing, and letting others into her internal world. She needed to reciprocate in relationships; she needed social and emo-tional connection, not new clothes or special foods.

In her first sessions of therapy, Megan was very reluctant and responded to my questions with one-word answers. After a few weeks of this, I said: "You know Megan, this time we have together is really your time, not mine. So I'd rather let you be in charge of it. It's totally up to you what we talk about for the next hour. If you don't want to talk, that's your choice, too." Megan looked up at me and made direct eye-contact; she seemed a little scared, but also curious. "Oh, okay," she said. She then looked down, for what seemed to be a very long time, and was silent. Suddenly and seemingly spontaneously, Megan began to tell me a few stories about the girls in the group. She was still uncomfortable and anxious for the hour to end, but nonetheless, she began to talk. I decided to keep this going and let it be the focus for our future sessions. I turned into the listener, becoming curious about everything she shared. I brought in none of my own ideas, opinions, or thoughts. Once, when I did bring up an "agenda item," she sunk back into her hole and relinquished the session to me.

When I explained this process to Megan's parents, they were pleased to learn that she was sharing, yet they knew she must be highly uncomfortable with it. They were anticipators, always talking for her, reading her cues, sensing what she needed or wanted, and always focused on her comfort. They let her stay in her room and be on the computer for hours, they bought her what she wanted; they were fearful of trying anything new. They clung to the connection they did have with her; however, at the same time, they didn't know how to impose any limits to elicit new behaviors from her. This was worrisome in light of her sexually provocative behavior. They knew they should bring it up, but were afraid she might talk less than she already was.

Megan's letters home were typical in what they contained. She demanded to come home. She wanted things—jeans, her cell phone, an iPod. She wasn't comfortable, she said. The letters had no emotional content. I coached her parents on letter writing to Megan and as a result they started to change their tone of voice. Rather than comforting and trying to meet Megan's needs, her parents began to ask more questions and did more reflecting. "Sounds like it is uncomfortable out there," they wrote. "Can you tell me more about it? We can't send you anything from home; what do you do for fun in your group? How are you coping with missing home? What is it like living outdoors?" Megan's parents began to engage in more dialogue and temporarily were forced out of their role as fixers.

As Megan settled into the program, she responded positively to the experiential and kinesthetic aspect of wilderness, and her external boundaries relaxed. She became a fifteen-year-old kid again. She had fun getting dirty, making fires at night, playing group games, and learning map and compass skills. Her persona switched from fashion-queen to tomboy. We also began to discover how funny she was. When Megan realized that she wasn't getting out of the program, she began to share more in her letters and answered her parents' questions. She still struggled with words connoting "feeling," but was able to talk about events and her experiences. Though still quiet compared to others, Megan was socializing in a new way and learning to solve problems, since the group had to work through conflicts every day. Her parents were enthused to see her vocabulary and ability to reveal things about herself grow and expand.

Throughout this time, her parents expressed a growing urge to talk on the phone—to hear Megan's voice. With mounting anticipation, we scheduled the first phone call and Megan and her parents were prepped on what to expect. Yet, within ten seconds, Megan's parents quickly resumed the old dynamic of anticipating wants and meeting needs. Megan was silent while her parents filled the empty space with questions, encouragement, and stories from home. When I asked her parents to let Megan respond, there was a long awkward silence. Finally, Megan spoke.

"Why can't I come home? Don't you think I've been here long enough?"

Her dad paused. "Well yes, we want you home, honey."

"I'm so dirty," Megan continued. "I need like a whole day in the tub to clean this dirt off. Also, I need new jeans. I think my legs have gotten bigger from all the hiking here, so I think my size changed. Plus, there are new ones from Abercrombie that I want."

Unsure of what to say, and feeling bad that she'd been living outside for five weeks, Megan's mom replied, "Okay, yes, sweetie."

"Where is my iPod? Can you bring it when you pick me up? Also I need to redo my nails; all the paint chipped off; you should see how dirty my hands are. You wouldn't believe it. . . . Also, where is my cell? Has anyone called?"

The requests continued until it was time to hang up and say "goodbye." This was the only template the family had for connecting.

REFRAMING

Reframing is a way of attuning, seeing, validating, and empowering your child to meet their own needs. It's a way of communicating the problem in a new way, by shifting the responsibility for the problem back onto the child.

In the scenario with Megan, both parents and child instantly grasped at the old status quo, because of its comfort and familiarity. This is understandable. Yet, with time, her parents could become effective at reframing and responding differently to Megan. They could enhance the glue, the emotional content, and intimacy in the parent–child relationship. Reframing includes reflective listening (taught in chapters five and nine), which is a skill used to enhance and draw out feelings and sharing in any conversation. Reframing, more specifically, is used when a child brings a problem to a parent, and the latter empowers the child to solve it.

THE STEPS FOR REFRAMING

1) Listen to your child closely and attune to the underlying emotion.
2) The underlying emotion and tone is more important than the content. The content may be the child wanting to come home, or get new clothes, or fighting over a cell phone. Engaging in the actual content is a way to get hooked and miss the real issue.
3) Mirror and reflect back to your child the underlying emotion.
4) Validate your child.
5) Keep yourself out of the problem, because when parents share

their opinions or thoughts, it's disempowering and often elicits a power-struggle.

6) Place problem-solving back with your child.

7) If your child continues to push the content, then set a boundary; but only after you've attuned to your child.

SOME EXAMPLES OF REFRAMING
(USING MEGAN'S CONVERSATION)

Example 1: Emotional attunement and reframing enhances the emotional content.

Megan: "Why can't I come home? Don't you think I've been here long enough?"

Dad: "Sweetie, you sound sad and upset, can you tell us what's wrong?" (*Attuning, while skipping content*)

Megan (*angrily*): "Yes, I'm mad that you sent me away."

Dad: "I hear that you're mad. I think I understand why you feel that way. Can you tell me more about it." (*Reflecting, validating, and putting it back onto her*)

Megan (*long pause*): "Well, I don't know. I just miss home. Being here feels like a punishment. I wish I could go back to my old school."

Dad: "You're right; this is a very difficult time. What's helped you to cope so far?" (*Validating, empowering her to solve her own problems*)

Megan: "I guess, talking to my group. The girls here are really cool—they understand."

Dad: "Well, sweetie, to tell you the truth, you sound well. You are sharing so much about what you're thinking and feeling. I can really see your progress." (*Finally, Dad shares his opinion, now that the tone has moved away from Megan wanting to be rescued. Ultimately, kids want their parents to see their progress.*)

Megan: "Thanks, Dad. I can't wait to see you."

Megan normally would never share her internal world with her parents. However, since her father kept reflecting and attuning, Megan didn't know what else to do but share more. The conversation circumvented Megan going into her wants and needs; instead, she and her father were able to share emotions and feel connected. Dad didn't interject, and Megan felt heard. As dad kept the focus on Megan, he was able to reframe the problem and let Megan be responsible for it. In addition, building this emotional connection with others was a critical component of her treatment; reframing further encouraged her maturation and individuation process.

Example 2: Reflecting and reframing is a way to avoid a power-struggle.

> **Megan**: "I'm so dirty. I need like a whole day in the tub to clean this dirt off. Also, I need new jeans. I think my legs have gotten bigger from all the hiking here, so I think my size changed. Plus, there are new ones from Abercrombie that I want."
>
> **Mom**: "You *are* really dirty, huh? How do you keep clean out there?" (*Reflecting and continuing to engage her*)
>
> **Megan**: "Well, we take these things called billy baths, which are basically sponge baths. It's pretty gross. But, Mom, I really do need new jeans."
>
> **Mom**: "I hear that you're frustrated and want new jeans. However, right now you can't wear jeans, so tell me more about your experience. What do you wear in the wilderness?" (*Attuning, reflecting, and engaging*)
>
> **Megan** (*after a pause*): "We wear actually pretty nice gear, and I have the warmest sleeping bag. But I'm still going to burn this stuff when I'm done. It reeks of smoke."
>
> **Mom**: "Oh, from the campfire? Have you learned how to make a fire?" (*And the sharing continues*)

Megan's mom successfully navigated away from Megan's demands. Through reflective listening, and engaging Megan in further dialogue by asking questions, she kept the focus on her child. With their inventiveness and savvy negotiating strategies, kids are masters of turning tables to avoid their own thoughts and feelings. Power-struggles are a means to the control that kids otherwise don't feel in their life. *Parents, in essence, have to train themselves to sidestep their child's schemes by avoiding content, and moving toward real dialogue, or sharing feelings.*

In the case of a power-struggle, if mom gets hooked by the content she can either agree to buy new jeans (same old pattern) or refuse by imposing a boundary. Here's an example of the mother setting a boundary *before she attuned* to her daughter, resulting in a power-struggle:

> **Megan**: "I'm so dirty. I need like a whole day in the tub to clean this dirt off. Also, I need new jeans. I think my legs have gotten bigger from all the hiking here, so I think my size changed. Plus, there are new ones from Abercrombie that I want."
>
> **Mom**: "Honey, can we please not talk about new jeans, you have so much clothing."
>
> **Megan** (*pause, with tension*): "You have no idea what I'm going through. I ask for the smallest thing. I haven't even been able to wear any of my own clothes for, like, five weeks—not even my own underwear. Do you know what that's like? You're still in our comfortable house every night, sleeping in a bed, not on the ground. You really don't get it, do you?"
>
> **Mom**: "Sorry, honey. Yes, we can get new jeans. I don't want to fight with you. I miss you so much."
>
> (*There is a long pause.*)
>
> **Mom**: "Have you made some friends?"
>
> (*Megan has shut down and only responds in one-word answers for the rest of the call.*)

Megan's mom got hooked by the content. Her lack of attunement shut down the sharing and further fueled their emotional divide. Kids want to feel heard, and Megan is used to feeling heard by getting something. She's replaying this well-known pattern; it's all she knows. Reframing helps keep the focus on Megan, to learn more about her feelings and experiences, and hopefully engage her in her own sharing. In this case, Megan genuinely wants to be seen and heard; she's not really fishing for a new pair of jeans.

BREAKING THE STEPS DOWN

1) Listen to your child closely and attune to the underlying emotion.
In the first step, it's essential that parents hone in on their child's emotions to assess what their child is feeling. For example, the statement of a child when he comes home from school and says, "I hate my school. It's the worst place ever; I never want to go there again," could stir up a lot of responses from a parent. In reframing, a parent's first job is to attune to the emotion. The mother looks at her son and attunes; he looks exhausted and drained. Or if not sure, a mother could ask, "Can you help me understand why you hate school?" to elicit if he feels frustrated or helpless about a grade, rejected by a friend, or some other emotion.

2) The underlying emotion and tone is more important than the content.
Most parents would get hooked by the content in the statement: "I hate my school. It's the worst place ever; I never want to go there again." The usual pattern of response from a rescuing parent would be, for example: "Sweetie, let me make you some popcorn and put in your favorite video." A lecturing parent might say: "Honey, you have to go to school. How can you hate it? You know you love science and soccer." A distracter parent might go into: "We're having dinner soon," and then begin talking to his sister while cooking.

These three examples show parents having an uncomfortable emotional response to the content of their child's statement and avoiding the emotion. These parents are hooked by the content of the child's issue. Moreover, these responses invalidate and undermine the child's emotions—which can cause further escalation.

3) Mirror and reflect back to your child the underlying emotion.
If a parent first attunes to the child, she can then reflect back the underlying emotion, to signal safety and receptivity.

> **Son**: "I hate my school. It's the worst place ever; I never want to go there again."
>
> **Mom**: "Sweetie, you look exhausted and drained." *(Attuning and mirroring)*
>
> **Son**: "I am."
>
> **Mom**: "What happened?"
>
> **Son**: "I stayed up way too late last night studying and I feel like I failed my test. This is so terrible."

Mom effectively skipped over the content, attuned, and mirrored back her child's emotion. The son shared as a response to his mother's attunement, and abruptly the content moved away from hating school.

4) Validate your child.

> **Son**: "I hate my school. It's the worst place ever; I never want to go there again."
>
> **Mom**: "Sweetie, you look exhausted and drained."
>
> **Son**: "I am."
>
> **Mom**: "What happened?"
>
> **Son**: "I stayed up way too late last night studying and I feel like I failed my test. This is so terrible."
>
> **Mom**: "That does sound terrible." (*Validating rather than making better*)
>
> **Son**: "Yeah, I know. It is!"

Most people want to make a situation better, smooth it over, or cheer someone up. Yet such responses undermine rather than validate the child's emotions. When parents validate their child's emotions, it sends the message: "I see you, I hear you, I understand." Happiness, sadness, fear, and anger—all these feelings are normal, human, and universal. Validation is simply saying, "I understand why you'd feel that way." Daniel Siegel writes:

> When our children tell us what they think or how they feel, it is important to respect their experience, whether or not it's the same as our own. Parents can listen to and understand their children's experience rather than tell them what they think and feel isn't valid.[20]

Furthermore, when parents validate their child's feelings, they let him stay with his feeling and give him permission to feel that way. The struggle, problem, or issue stays in the child's lap.

5) Keep yourself out of the problem.
It's disempowering and often elicits a power-struggle when parents share their opinions or thoughts. When parents refrain from adding their own thoughts and feelings, it forces the conversation to stay with the child's discomfort and struggle. Moreover, the minute the parent shares anything from his or her own perspective, it creates an opportunity for the child to oppose the parent (which happens easily if the child is angry), or look more actively to the parent to solve the issue. In all cases, the parent inserting himself reliably stops the child sharing further and allows her to avoid responsibility for problem-solving. Here's an example of parents empathically attempting to reassure, assuage, or encourage their child; yet all attempts fall short, because they're undermining or rescuing.

> **Dad**: "I hated school, too, but I stuck with it."
> **Son** (*walking to his room*): "Well, I'm not you. . . ."
> **Mom**: "I'm sure you did great on your test."

Son: "Yeah right, Mom! How would you know?"

Mom: "You can't really mean that. I know you love school."

Son: "You don't know anything. You have to fix it now. It's your fault."

The parents are skipping over their child's emotional urgency. In essence, their message is: "Your feelings don't matter." When parents tell their child what they believe, they're not listening or attuning and are actually short-circuiting further sharing and connection. Unknowingly and indirectly, parents undermine and further alienate their child's emotions. When kids ascertain this truth, situations can escalate to where the child further directs anger and frustration back at the parent. At this point, parents have lost the reframe.

6) Allow your child to solve the problem.

Son: "I hate my school. It's the worst place ever; I never want to go there again."

Mom: "Sweetie, you look exhausted and drained. (*Attuning*)

Son: "I am."

Mom: "What happened?"

Son: "I stayed up way too late last night studying and I feel like I failed my test. This is so terrible."

Mom: "That does sound terrible." (*Validating*)

Son: "Yeah, I know. It is!"

Mom: "Do you want to talk about it more?" (*Leaving son in charge of problem*)

Son: "No. I guess I will just wait to see what grade I get."

Mom: "Okay. I'm here if you want to talk more." (*Showing emotional support*)

In this case, mom refrains from sharing her own thoughts or opinions because the problem is not hers to solve. Instead, she sends the message: "I know you can handle it, so I'm not going to get involved."

Other statements that keep the responsibility for the problem in the child's lap are:

- "How do you want to proceed?"
- "How will you cope with this?"
- "What do you think you're going to do?"
- "What's next?"
- "What helps when you feel this way?"
- "What do you think about this problem?"

These are ways of empowering kids and keeping them in charge of their own problem-solving.

7) If your child continues to push the content, then you can set a boundary, but only after you have attuned to your child.
For this last step, which hopefully parents will be able to circumvent by following the previous ones, I offer two examples. Sometimes kids are extremely persistent, and want to win their negotiation or power-struggle at all costs, even when mom and dad are attuning.

EXAMPLE 1

Son: "I hate my school. It's the worst place ever; I never want to go there again."

Mom: "Sweetie, you look exhausted and drained."

Son: "I am."

Mom: "What happened?" (*Attuning*)

Son: "Nothing. I hate it there. I just never want to go back."

Mom: "You sound really upset and frustrated. Do you want to talk about it?" (*Attuning and engaging*)

Son: "No. I refuse to go to school tomorrow."

Mom: "I can see that something's wrong. I'm here if you want to talk about it." (*Reflecting, showing support*)

Son: "I don't want to talk about it!"

Mom: "Okay, I hear that you don't want to talk about it. However, I can't really understand why you feel so strongly and don't want to go back to school unless you share more. I think you know school is non-negotiable. I'm here though if you want to talk." (*Reflecting and setting a boundary*)

(*The son goes to his room.*)

EXAMPLE 2

Daughter (*with tension in her voice*): "Dad, my cell phone is terrible. I really need a new one. I can never get coverage with this one."

Dad: "You sound upset. What happened?" (*Attuning while avoiding the content*)

Daughter (*angrily*): "Well, it keeps cutting off when I talk to. . . . I mean, nothing. Aren't you listening? I said that I don't have coverage. I want a new phone!"

Dad: "Jenny, I hear that you're really mad about your cell phone and not getting coverage when you talk. Did something specific happen?" (*Reflecting, engaging*)

Daughter: "No, Dad. Can I get a new one? Please."

Dad: "I'm sorry to hear about your frustration. Perhaps we can take it down to the store and get it checked out." (*Since his daughter is not sharing, Dad cannot validate an emotion, but he does show compassion.*)

Daughter: "No, Dad. I just want a new one. The other company has better coverage."

Dad: "Sorry, Jenny. We're not switching phone companies or getting new phones. Let me know if you want to go down to the store. I'm happy to go with you." (*Sets a boundary yet keeps problem-solving in his daughter's lap*)

Sometimes kids don't want to solve problems; they just want to get their way. Ultimately, parents need to set limits, but doing so is most effective after they've attuned to their children and worked to reframe the problem. It sounds like Jenny is upset about a phone call she had and is focusing on getting a new phone, rather than talking about what's bothering her. At the end of the day, parents can only control their responses to their kids; parents cannot control their child's thoughts, emotions, or actions. It's okay to set limits and let your child feel his or her frustration.

Remember: struggle is good. If parents want their kids to develop internal resources, they have to let them do their own problem-solving. With this approach, parents are consciously breaking out of their habitual patterns and intentionally reframing issues. That is all parents can control.

chapter 9

BRINGING YOUR CHILD HOME

Skills for Reintegration

SURPRISINGLY—OR PERHAPS not—throughout my years of experience with adolescents, only rarely did a client share a story of a fight with a parent that was repaired or resolved. Most families that get stuck don't turn toward each other after fights; they keep moving farther and farther apart. Families pretend to move on, avert conflict, and resume roles and patterns, only for the conflict to happen again.

These dynamics become set and ingrained as the patterns of moving away and avoiding feelings are reinforced. When I've listened to adolescents talk about the problems and conflicts in their relationships with their parents, the image that comes to mind is a fortress of misunderstanding, with castle walls nestled within others, all surrounded by a moat, that keeps an adolescent apart from a parent, making it impossible for them to connect.

Every family has conflict. After decades of research on relationships, and his own clinical experience, John Gottman concluded that families that weathered conflicts and storms effectively are the families that "turn toward" each other.[21] Families that have honed the skills of attunement and respond to each other's bids for connection have the tools to overcome obstacles and navigate conflicts. For parents of adolescents to respond effectively to cues, they need to identify and attune to underlying emotions, not just fix problems. When parents engage in the patterns described in the previous chapters or lack their own self-awareness, their attunement to their child is also lost as a consequence.

How do families learn to "turn toward" rather than away from each other emotionally? How do parents stay emotionally receptive without rescuing their teens? I've already discussed ways for parents to identify and *own* their own patterns (not your child's problem) and begin to take responsibility; let go of their set opinions and begin to enhance their own self-awareness; learn the art of reframing and empower their child to problem-solve. What come next are the nuts and bolts of navigating a new relationship with your child. Parents can learn skills to sidestep the old traps and dead-ends they frequently fell into before their child was sent to treatment.

After their child has completed treatment and is transitioning to a boarding school, is resuming college, or is coming home, parents are abruptly thrown back into a hands-on relationship with her. This can be startling and may come with mixed feelings. Parents feel joy and relief, yet many also feel fear and dread. Understandably, they're worried that their child will relapse into making poor choices, reconnecting with negative peers, or resuming addictions. More significantly, parents are haunted by the fear of returning to the old parent–child relationship, which was fraught with manipulation, lies, power-struggles, negotiations, and overall discord. Parents can also relapse and return to old patterns, too.

One problem is that the parents experienced very little of the tremendous strides their teenager took in wilderness therapy; they may not have seen the growth in his interpersonal skills and self-awareness. In addition, when kids call or visit home, maintaining their new maturity is tentative at best. Kids want to let down and just *be* in front of their parents, something that involves varying levels of regression. Complaining, venting, snapping, bargaining, blaming, and manipulation can resume quickly. Parents frequently report that their child was mature and responsible in the parent workshop, yet when they got in the car to go to lunch, it seemed to vanish in an instant.

This unraveling, albeit disappointing, is fairly predictable. Yet I challenge parents to reflect on their own behavior when they visit their own father and mother. They, too, can still fall into the same emotional traps and can feel similar dynamics they felt at age twelve. We're vulnerable to our parents and it can bring out childlike behavior. This should be expected. Where parents need to focus with their child transitioning home is making this regression into an opportunity to practice their skills that this chapter outlines.

ASSERTIVE COMMUNICATION: THE "I FEEL" STATEMENT

After parents become more attuned to their emotions, the next step is for them to communicate their feelings. Rather than acting them out using obsolete patterns such as lecturing, blaming, avoidance, and rescuing, parents can instead share and communicate assertively. Doing so enhances the emotional dialogue in the home, creates openings for more intimate conversations, and further legitimizes the importance of understanding each other. Parents repeatedly get mad at their kids when they push or violate boundaries: being late for curfew, lying, failing to follow through, and so on. Yet, rarely do they actually share how they feel.

If, for instance, their child comes home at 12:30 and his curfew was eleven, parents might say one of the following:

- "How can you do this, you don't live in a hotel."
- "You could have been killed staying out this late."
- "I thought you were trying to show us you'd changed."
- "Where were you? Why didn't you answer your phone?"
- "You're in big trouble."

All these statements can readily escalate into more conflict—further disrupting dialogue. Additionally, it's unlikely your child will express remorse or guilt after feeling lectured or blamed. What parents are encouraged to do instead is to give an "I feel" statement:

- I feel _____ (sad, worried, frustrated, scared, hopeful, angry, happy, etc.)
- I feel this way when _____ (event)
- I feel this way because I think _____ (your thoughts about the event)
- My hope for myself is _____ (your actions)
- My hope for you is _____ (other's actions)

Example #1

"I feel worried and scared when you come home this late. I feel this way, because all I think about when you're not home at night is all the bad things that can happen to you. I hope I can really communicate to you how important it is that you're home at a safe hour. I also hope you can respect my boundaries."

Example #2

"I feel powerless when you don't come home at curfew and I can't reach you on the phone. I feel this way because I think we've put so much energy into repairing our relationship and rebuilding trust and it's discouraging not to know what to do. My hope for myself is that I can share this with you rather than just yell. My hope for you is that you can really understand how it impacts me, and how important it is that we talk through things."

Example #3

"I feel angry, but underneath that I guess I feel hurt. I feel hurt when you disregard our rules and boundaries. I feel this way because I think you may be doing this on purpose to hurt us. My hope is that I can follow through on what I say I'll do in rebuilding our relationship. My hope for you is that you too will follow through."

All these statements require a degree of composure and clarity of mind. If you're too churned-up as a parent, you'll need to take a time-out (discussed below)—decompress, gather your thoughts, or even wait until the morning. What's critical is that you assertively communicate what you feel. All the above examples offer openings for real dialogue. You're letting your child know how his actions impact others, specifically you. After sharing thoughts and feelings, you still need to give consequences, but only after thoughts and feelings are shared. For example, the consequence for violating a curfew might be that your child cannot go out the following night. It's crucial to have a "behavior contract" in place (see Appendix), before your child transitions home so all expectations are clear in advance. That means when your child walks in the door late, the consequence is explicit and has been agreed to beforehand.

"I" STATEMENTS NOT "YOU" STATEMENTS

The five essential components to the "I feel" statement—feeling, event, thought, and hope for self and other—form a whole. Realistically, though, it can be challenging to remember all the parts. In an effort to avoid parents getting thrown off and sidestepping it all together, the essence of the statement is the first sentence, "I feel _____" (emotion). This statement is imperative because it steers parents away from "You" statements, which are frequently resorted to in a conflict: "You're late again," "You're being disrespectful," "You're not following through," "You're doing this to me," "You're never going to change."

Embedded within the "You" statement is blame. The natural response to blame is to close oneself off, defend, and prepare for a rebuttal. It stunts further dialogue, shutting the door to hearing each others' thoughts and feelings. At a core place, kids want to be heard as much as parents do: the best way to be heard is to communicate effectively with "I" statements. Parents cannot control their child's choices, yet they can share their feelings in an assertive and direct way, and also respond differently.

Lastly, essential to the "I" statement, is the *I* itself. Parents are taking responsibility for their own emotions and experience, thus breaking their habitual patterns. In every "I" statement is an expression of accountability and self-awareness. Above, I gave three examples of emotional responses parents might have: scared and worried, powerless and discouraged, and angry and hurt. Kids need to understand the subtlety of their parents' feelings and responses; they need to take in the individuality of each parent.

With feedback, teens can become more aware of and attuned to others, and develop empathy. There's a whole range of responses possible for a child being out until 12:30 a.m., but your child won't know yours unless you tell her. This process enhances emotional dialogue, making it permissible to feel and express emotions in the home.

REFLECTIVE LISTENING:
CREATING A SAFE PLACE FOR YOUR CHILD

Ultimately, we want kids to share their thoughts and feelings and turn toward us as parents. We want to hear all the uncomfortable stuff, because it's much healthier for children, adolescents, and young adults to share their thoughts and feelings instead of shutting down, using substances, or engaging in self-harming behaviors. Reflective listening is a reliable approach to attune to your child compassionately while also creating emotional safety. Active listening goes a long way in healthy communication, and can be restorative and healing because the other person feels *seen* and *heard*.

Parents need to be approachable, to communicate, in essence, "I'm here and I want to listen." The objective in reflective listening is to mirror back the key components of the "I feel" statement: the feelings, events, and thoughts. In reflecting, allow your child to exhaust all thoughts and feelings until there's a natural impulse to shift focus, or ask for your thoughts. Let your child stay with his or her feelings: honor them. Don't interrupt, fix, or try to cheer your child up. Here are some examples of reflective listening:

Example #1

Daughter: "Mom, I feel terrible. All I want to do is drink again. I'm really scared. I feel this way when I see Jenna and she's drinking wine. I feel this way because I think that I can't do it. I can't be sober forever." (*Kids may or may not use the whole "I feel" statement.*)

Mother: "Sweetie, I hear that you're feeling terrible; that you're scared and want to use again; and that you feel this when Jenna is drinking, and don't think you can do it. That you can't be sober forever. Is there more?"

Daughter: "Yeah, I feel kind of hopeless again. Kind of depressed."

Mother: "I hear that you're also feeling hopeless and depressed."

Daughter (*long pause*): "But in a way, I don't want to be like Jenna—you know. She isn't going anywhere with her life. I guess I've been there, done that."

Mother: "Sounds like you have some new perspectives now."

Daughter: "Yeah, I guess. What do you think? Do you think I can be sober?" (*Natural shift*)

Mother: "Well, I think that you are sober, and it seems like you are talking about your difficult feelings, rather than drinking."

Daughter: "Yeah, I guess. Thanks, Mom."

When kids bring up complicated feelings, it's best to stay in the reflective-listening role. When they ask for your opinion, it's best to be empathic and supportive. If parents interject their own thoughts, opinions, and fears, the child can easily shift out of his own process and target the parent.

Example #2

Son: "Dad, I feel frustrated. I feel this when you never have a beer in the house, anymore. It's like you still don't trust me. Come on! It's the Super Bowl. Have a beer, Dad."

Father: "Tim, I hear that you're frustrated that I'm not drinking and relaxing with a beer—especially with today being the Super Bowl. I also hear that when I don't drink, you feel that I don't trust you. Is that right?"

Son: "Yeah, Dad. Come on! I've been home, like, over a month now. Are you just going to stop drinking forever? I mean, I had the problem, not you."

Father: "I hear that you're upset and that you don't understand why I stopped drinking."

Son: "Well, it feels like you're doing it to like rub it in my face."

Father: "I hear you saying that when I chose to stop drinking it feels like I'm rubbing your problem in your face. Am I getting this right?

Son: "Something like that."

Father: "Well, I really appreciate you sharing this and telling me how you feel. I had no idea that it was impacting you that way. Really, it was just a choice I made personally. Your mother still will have a glass of wine. But for me, knowing what you went through, I'm not comfortable casually having a beer. That's just me. I don't know how else to explain it. I'm not saying I'll never have a beer again. But we've been through a lot as a family and right now, really, I have no desire to drink. It just tastes terrible to me. So, I by no means am trying to hurt you, and I'm happy that you're telling me how you feel."

Son: "Okay, I think I get it."

Example #3

Son: "Mom, I'm so mad at my professor. I think she's going to give me an 'F.' I'm so angry. I know she doesn't like me. She's targeting me because I went away to a program. So what if I handed in a few homeworks late?"

Mother: "I hear that you're really angry. That you feel your professor doesn't like you and is targeting you because you went to a treatment program. You think you might get an 'F' for handing in homeworks late?"

Son: "Yeah, ugh. So frustrating. I mean what am I supposed to do? She thinks I'm just a stoner."

Mother: "You sound really frustrated. You feel that she just sees you the same old way. Am I understanding you right?"

Son: "Well, I don't know. But it sure feels that way. What will you think if I fail?"

Mother: "Well, it affects you much more than me. But truthfully, I feel concerned when I see you blaming others. I feel this way because I think you play a large role in whatever grade you get. My hope for myself is that I'll let you solve it. My hope for you is that you see that you can only control your part, your behavior, which includes handing your assignments in. You cannot control how she sees you."

(The son is quiet.)

Mother: "I appreciate you sharing with me. And I hope you can tell me how it goes."

Son: "Okay."

This is an example where a mother shares an "I feel" statement after reflective listening. Parents may want to make their feelings more clear, especially if their child asks for their opinion. In this case, the mother keeps the responsibility with her son, yet shares the way she feels her son is contributing to the problem.

IN ALL THESE instances, the emotional content the son or daughter is sharing may be uncomfortable for parents. Some parents might become critical, defensive, and try to rescue, or simply stop the conversation. Others might think reflective listening sounds strange. It seems awkward to repeat what your child said.

Reflective listening also involves more than just repeating back the words; body language and non-verbal communication are fundamental. Eye-contact, stopping what you're doing, and sitting near your child show that you're listening and attuning. Looking up rather than down at your child creates a feeling of safety and signals that she has your full attention. Sitting on the floor of your child's room or on a couch while he's standing are ways to convey receptivity. Kids may feel intimidated and less likely to share when you stand above them. Likewise, not crossing your arms and legs, opening your chest, and facing your child suggest openness. Your facial expressions should also mirror empathy and compassion. Lastly, you should use an inquisitive and receptive tone of voice. In this way, you're communicating: "It's safe to share your feelings with me."

Still, you might think, "This isn't going to work with my child." I challenge you to try it with your spouse, partner, or a friend. You'll be surprised how nice it is to be reflected, to truly know the other person is listening. You can be a safe outlet for your child and be the role model for healthy ways to talk about complex subjects. It's a gift for your child to share with you; they're employing the skills they learned in treatment, as opposed to turning away and acting out. Parents can support, encourage, and validate these skills.

TIME-OUTS

Time-outs are an essential tool for parents and kids alike. There are many circumstances where it's not appropriate or safe to share feelings, such as when kids are emotional and reactive or parents are angry and tense. Timing is critical for open and receptive conversations, which means that parents, young adults, and adolescents need breaks. A time-out may be taken in a moment of fury, where a parent or child removes him- or herself from the conflict. It may also include pausing and *not* discussing an issue or conflict until the following day. Having an interlude is often essential for emotional clarity and to allow family members to move into listening and away from blaming roles.

Most kids hate time-outs. They associate them with being three years old and being told to go to their room after a tantrum. However, the time-outs I'm describing are fundamentally different in the sense they're self-imposed, elective breaks. It's vital for parents to model healthy time-outs. For example: "I know I can't discuss this right now. I'm too emotional and too upset to be able to talk or listen. I'm going to go for a walk. I'd like to be able to talk about this in an hour." Or, "I'm too tired to talk through this tonight; I know I'm feeling upset, but I want to sleep on it and talk in the morning." A parent who's about to yell at his son who's been caught in a lie, might pause and instead simply say: "I need to take a break right now." Chances are that when a parent models time-outs, kids will emulate. Parents are saying through their actions, "I need to manage my emotions; I need to work at it, too, not just you."

What differentiates a time-out from shutting down or withdrawing is that a time-out is intentional and communicated. A parent is clearly stating, "I need a break." A parent or child is disengaging in the heat of the moment and then reengaging; the break implies a coming back together. When the appropriate amount of time has lapsed, parents need to initiate repairing, which means resuming "I feel" statements and reflective listening.

SETTING BOUNDARIES

As we saw with the cows in the pasture, individuals of all ages push up against boundaries to know what the parameters are that each individual needs to operate within. This is human nature. In spite of their pushing against structure and testing limits, children love routine, order, even rules, because it creates predictability, which in turn promotes a feeling of safety.

Developmentally, kids feel safe within defined boundaries. When adolescents travel outside them through experimentation, defiance, impulsivity, peer pressure, and so on, they might feel excitement and grandiosity, yet they can also feel unsafe and anxious. When a teen steps out of bounds, it's as though nobody is watching; this can be exhilarating but also anxiety-provoking. Frequently, the escalation of adolescent behavior is often actually the teen wanting to get caught. Parents shockingly discover this truth:

- "He left the vodka bottle on the floor of his room, and of course he knew I'd find it."
- "She left her journal spread open on her bed, describing her sexual experiences. It was almost like she left it for me."
- "She cuts her arms and then wears long sleeves, but it seems she pushes her sleeves up strategically for me to see and know she is cutting again."
- "He really didn't cover up the lie very well. It was almost like he didn't care about getting caught."

Because struggling young people may not have the emotional wherewithal, internal resources, or communication skills to ask for help, the escalation of behavior and pushing boundaries to an extreme force the parents to intervene. It's almost like children are screaming, "I NEED HELP!" At these times, typically kids feel out of control internally; they don't know how to stop their behavior and aren't in a rational place. What they need most is for someone else to contain them; they need to be managed and regulated externally. Through suicidal gestures, binge-drinking, overdosing, running away, and refusing to go to school, kids have wandered so far beyond the realm of normal behavior that eventually they get everybody's attention.

When your child comes home, it's critical you reinstate the boundaries and expectations of the home. This includes specifics like eating dinners together, establishing household chores, setting curfews, having family meetings, providing expectations for school, and relating consequences. If an adolescent stays sober, finishes high school, or keeps a job, these behaviors will bring positive natural consequences, like emotional maturity, a diploma, or earned money. Parents can, therefore, grant more freedoms when a child has built up trust, such as having access to the car, staying out later, or earning more money.

Negative consequences for not abiding by the contract (see Appendix) or expectations may mean fewer freedoms, restrictions on use of the car, less time outside the home, and the cutting of the allowance. When parents set lucid and clear boundaries and consequences, they're taking a step closer to reducing negotiations and conflict in the house. The more that's laid out beforehand, the more parents simply have to enforce and rely on the contract. At the end of the day, these choices are up to your child; the consequences for their actions impart life lessons.

If parents continue to avoid boundaries, fall prey to manipulations, and fail to follow through with consequences, the message they send their child is, "What I say doesn't really matter and you can negotiate anything, if you try hard enough."

FAMILY CHECK-INS

In working toward integrating your child's gains into the family, family check-ins can help cultivate connection and closeness. One mother I worked with used this skill after her son transitioned home from rehab. "It's a tough road for him because he has no healthy peers yet," she told me. "He still seems slightly depressed. He's reconnected with only one friend who is supportive of his sobriety, though I'm not sure if he's smoking pot or not. But I'll tell you, Krissy, he's very open and affectionate and we never had that before. He'll talk about everything and always hugs us and says, 'I love you.'"

This was heartening to hear; prior to treatment this young man had barely talked to his parents and lied constantly. His mother was so shaky when it came to issues of trust that she felt on edge and frantic whenever she had the slightest doubt. For her, the situation felt like post-traumatic stress disorder (PTSD): a result of being lied to so many times. Yet the emotional closeness she felt with her son was like a salve for her frayed nerves; it felt genuine. She knew her son would have ups and downs transitioning home, yet she felt like she had new ground under her feet with this new ability to talk openly. She made a point of creating space for check-ins every night—to share feelings and be present, if her son wanted to talk.

Family check-ins are simply creating space to talk, share, and explore feelings. For some, sharing might be summed up in one word: "sad," "tired," "overwhelmed," "content." For others, it could lead to hours of talking. Some kids won't come to their parents with "I feel" statements. Parents can initiate this process and safeguard this nightly ritual. They can also use the opportunity to share their own feelings, which may or may not relate to their child. Moreover, if you're worried about your child who has recently transitioned home, the check-in may be a safe place to bring it up. An example: "Sarah, I'm concerned that you may be staying up too late, because you seem so tired during the day." Creating space for sharing feelings allows families to turn toward each other through the difficulties.

MISTAKES AND ACCOUNTABILITY: WHY MISTAKES ARE IMPORTANT

For most parents, the old parent–child relationship is so filled with wounds and sore subjects that they don't know where to step. Every parent is terrified of making mistakes. Once your child is in treatment and on the right path, many parents are afraid to say the wrong thing, mess things up, or make their child mad. On their first phone call, or during their first family visit, parents are frequently like deer caught in headlights, frozen and worried. They fret, "What if I go right back to my pattern and say the wrong thing?" or "I really don't want to have our old fights," or "I just want it to go well and get along."

We're all human, and parents and kids are going to make mistakes. I tell parents to expect to say the wrong thing and upset their child and be tongue-tied. However, I also say to parents that with hard work it is possible as a family to move into a new place with insight and awareness; but that doesn't mean the old habits don't exist. Most family visits are met with some new and some old interactions, a mix of positive and negative moments. The process of integrating these changes will take time and trial and error.

More positively, I tell parents that mistakes are good in that they provide an opportunity to practice one's emotional work and accountability to have new outcomes. For example, if a mother impulsively goes to comfort her adolescent son when he wells up in tears, and tells him that she wants to take him out for ice cream (this may sound silly, but it happens), she's acting out her pattern again. However, she also has an opportunity. She may not catch it in that moment or even that day; but she can always repair it and take accountability if she's genuinely on the path to breaking her pattern.

So, for example, even a week later she could say: "You know, sweetie, when you cried at the family visit and I started talking about ice cream, I wasn't really listening to you and understanding your sadness. I was rescuing you again; I was trying to make it better. What I realize is that I need to become more comfortable with your sadness. Really, I was rescuing myself because it's uncomfortable for me to see you in pain and sad. I want you to know that I'm working on this." Frequently, parents console and rescue their struggling children because they feel uncomfortable and intolerant. This mother may have replayed an old pattern, but because of her new awareness she also had a new outcome with her son.

Mistakes are an opportunity. Nobody changes overnight and nobody is going to do it perfectly every time. The goal is to continue owning your pattern and working at it. We can't expect kids to be perfect, either. Parents are often fearfully waiting for their child to mess up; they're so accustomed to their child's negative behavior that it takes time to rebuild trust. This concept of accountability is an ongoing practice for parents and kids alike. For example, another boy I worked with pushed himself to total honesty. He said to his parents at a visit:

"Mom and Dad, you know how I wrote a letter of accountability? Well, I still kept things out. This is hard to say because I told you that that letter was the whole truth; so I feel like I'm lying twice now. But the truth is, I still have kept things from you. I did steal your earrings, Mom, for money to buy pot. I did steal alcohol from the house, Dad. Although I admitted my addiction to you, it is very hard to admit that I stole from you. I also took money from your purse, Mom. I took tens mostly, hoping you wouldn't notice. But I did that a lot. So I just want to own it now and that is the whole truth."

This is excruciating for parents to hear; yet they have to acknowledge that their child is turning toward them. Rather than fearing mistakes, parents can model that it's okay to mess up; the goal is to own your behavior and keep moving forward to break patterns, to stay connected as a family.

Routinely creating space to see and hear your child while communicating in a way that both validates and nurtures your child's development toward becoming an independent adult is the path. It's hard, but works if families stick to it. When parents and kids know how to talk about their patterns and feelings, when they have the resources, and communication and listening skills to navigate future conflicts and problems, it's likely families will stay connected through challenging times. Meanwhile, the more that parents can own their own mistakes and model emotional maturity, the more they'll be able to guide and nurture the positive development of their child.

chapter 10

OPENING TO THE FUTURE

FOR KIDS IN treatment, persisting in old habits is not viable, which is why most programs apply pressure to shake up stagnant behavior. Many young people in treatment find themselves outside their "comfort zone." A shut-down adolescent might find it excruciating to sit through group and individual therapy without uttering a word, knowing that sharing is the only way to advance through the program. Yet parents at home are still in the same environment, with the same distractions that reinforce old habits and provide ways to close off emotions. Nonetheless, opportunities exist to wake up and address the emotional slumber that plagues many adults and prevents them from attuning to their child.

An out-of-control teen and the resulting chaos in the home often spark change. If nothing else, they surely get everybody's attention. Salvador Minuchin, a pioneer in family therapy, once said that kids who act out are the barometer of the family, the escape valve for all the pressure that has built up.[22] It's easy to focus on the child being the problem; yet looking for simple solutions rarely produces the needed systemic change. If the child is the messenger, parents should slow down and read the message.

As we've seen, for parents to open up to pain, discomfort, and uncertainty—which is essentially what is required of them—can be very hard. It's human nature to want to avoid pain and build walls to protect oneself; marriages may not be able to sustain such friction. However, the sacred, unconditional nature of the parent–child bond can propel parents to wake up, employ new skills, and embrace the lessons. Opening up to feelings and becoming vulnerable can be heart-wrenching and grief-filled; yet they can also allow parents to see their child, and perhaps the world, anew.

GRACE

Grace, a local news broadcaster, and Peter had been married for twenty years when the car Peter was driving home late one night hit a tree, and he died. Peter had a history of drinking too much, emotional avoidance was the norm in the home, and the reality of his drinking was safely tucked away in the family's vault. People wondered whether he'd been reckless or had taken his life. Grace had known her husband was under a lot of stress at work and in the home with their older son drifting from the family. However, she couldn't wrap her mind around alcoholism or suicide. He wasn't like that, she told herself. Or was he?

As you might expect, Peter's death dismantled the entire family. Grace felt she had to put her own grieving on hold to aid her reeling children. One son, Winston, was already oppositional, defiant, and using drugs. He'd been through drug court and was required to attend the substance-abuse counseling program, though the only pieces of knowledge Winston gained from it were new drug dealers' phone numbers. Winston went on a drug binge shortly after the funeral and, after getting his stomach pumped, was sent off to a wilderness program. Grace was a wreck.

Peter and Grace's youngest child, Bella, aged twelve, was strongly introverted and always by her mother's side. Bella was like a sponge, soaking up the energy and emotions of others. The combination of her father's death, brother's tumult, and mother's denial was more than she could take. She was sweet and well-liked, but she wasn't particularly good at anything. In the two years following her father's death, Bella slowly drifted toward adopting a "Goth" persona as a way to express the difficult emotions that were plaguing her. She listened to depressive music, dressed in black, wore heavy eye make-up, and hung out with kids like her.

With time, she also began another behavior called self-mutilation. One night, listening alone to her dreary music and feeling overwhelmed because her mother had gone on a date, Bella unthinkingly grabbed a lighted candle and put it to her skin and burned her forearm. Though seemingly wrong, she smiled. She felt different, a sense of control. That a physical pain could take the place of the emotional one was a revelation.

Meanwhile, Grace had cemented over all her emotions and had mastered the art of denial. She clung to any normalcy—her job and routine, her glasses of wine and evening shows, her Ambien. She began dating to further aid her distraction. Winston was getting better and was now applying for colleges; but Grace knew something was askew with Bella. However, Grace was buried too deep to look and see that her once-little girl was now lost to the Gothic underworld. She let Bella be; after all, Bella was grieving and it was appropriate to wear black.

Bella's discovery of the candle became a nightly ritual. It helped her escape all the heaviness that she didn't know how to filter out. By now, the notion that she was really f——ed up weighed her down. She felt stuck because she didn't want to renounce her habit, but at the same time she was afraid to continue it. Whether intentionally or not, one night Bella burned the cuff on her shirt and it caught fire. The fire raced up the sleeve; Bella screamed and ran to the bathroom as fast as she could to douse it with water. Her mother, still awake, jumped out of bed to see what the commotion was.

Grace stepped into the bathroom and froze. She'd reached her turning point; her dam had finally broken. She'd effectively denied her sadness and pain related to Winston, and her grief and despair from her husband's death. But seeing her little girl's self-inflicted burn-marks up and down both arms was not something she could contain. Grace grabbed Bella, and taking in the gravity of what was happening, they both began to wail.

For the first time, they grieved. They cried for the terrible loss of a father and a husband. They cried for Winston; they cried for Bella's arms. They cried for each other's isolation and all the empty space that had come to fill their relationship. They cried for all the feelings they'd put away: the grief, rage, hurt, sadness, anger, and powerlessness. They made a vow to face it all, to open up to all their feelings, and become healthy and close again. The scars on Bella's arms came to represent how far their denial had taken them. They swore to each other that enough was enough. That night, Bella took her stuffed animals and slept in her mother's bed, along with Grace. She woke up the next day and put on a pink sweatshirt and jeans and, hand in hand, she and her mom went to see a grief counselor.

Bella continued to feel sucked in by her gloomy peer group. She decided that she was too afraid she might resume some self-harming habit (she knew other kids that used razors) and asked Grace if she could be sent away like Winston to a therapeutic school to be with other kids on a journey to health. Grace understood.

With her husband gone, Winston at college, and Bella at the school, Grace had nowhere to hide. Everywhere she looked, there was pain. She knew on the surface her life appeared a failure—one husband dead and two children in treatment. Yet she was tired of feeling dead inside; she wanted to wake up and feel alive. Still, she was terrified. She worried about how others saw her and that she might go crazy. Nonetheless, at the same time she felt a strong urge to explore the edginess, uncertainty, and rawness she felt in everyday life. In fact, Grace was so scared of what denial did to her, that she moved toward anything that slightly bothered her and opened herself up to it. Her comfort zone of denial had become unbearable.

Through her own treatment plan, outlined by her grief counselor,

Grace courageously explored her own uncharted territory. She started some practical exercises, like tuning into her feelings and emotions on a day-to-day, moment-to-moment basis through journaling. With her therapist, she began to explore her history of denying, shutting down, and turning away emotions. She practiced new skills like reflective listening, assertive communication, and opening to feelings.

Grace also joined a meditation group in her church to further focus on inner calm and breathwork. The group emphasized becoming more observant of the delicate nature of life, to revel in everyday beauty: a flower in bloom, birdsong, a child's smile. During her meditations, she remembered Winston's letters from his wilderness program, where he'd come to appreciate the smallest things:

> Mom, out here we have so little, it makes me realize how lucky I was to have a hot shower in the morning, or a fridge full of food. But I am also realizing that we don't even need that stuff either—here I actually love cold granola with oats, and beans and rice cooked on the fire. At home, I was either using drugs, scheming to get drugs, or playing video games and stuff; I never noticed anything around me. I have learned all the trees here and it is the best to sleep under quaking Aspens—also Juniper and Sage bark is the perfect nesting to make a fire. It is all really cool. It is amazing how self-sufficient I feel.

Grace, too, came to know the secret truth that noticing the small things is the richness in life. She also found support through strengthening her ties to the community.

Grace didn't know what the future would bring, or what each new moment would have in store, but she wanted to be alert and open to it. She courageously exposed her fears about Winston and Bella's future, armed with the wisdom of her own personal experience: we're all stronger than what happens to us. The positive outcome of so much therapy was that she came to have a common language of sharing feelings about the rawness of life with her kids. Moreover, the vulnerability that Grace, Winston, and Bella came to know intimately allowed them to access life and share feelings openly.

Grace began to embrace everything that happened to her, good and bad. She became more confident and fearless about the future. Rather than putting on armor and protection, she lived from her own vulnerability. We all have the ability to evolve and, instead of fearing life and closing off from it, to see every obstacle on the path as providing an opportunity to learn and grow.

FORGIVENESS

The remaining steps in repairing the fractured relationships between parents and an adolescent and young adult who've gone through the treatment process are forgiveness and gratitude. Touching their own vulnerability allows parents to forgive themselves and their child. They can let go of their feelings of failure, humiliation, anger, hurt, embarrassment, and shame. Moreover, parents need to have compassion for themselves as parents. Parenthood is the most demanding, taxing, arduous job there is. As Henry T. Close writes:

> There is no question that our parents failed us as parents. All parents fail their children, and ours were no exception. No parent is ever adequate enough for the job of being a parent, there is no way not to fail at it. No parent ever has enough love, or wisdom, or maturity, or patience. No parent ever succeeds completely. As kids we needed more mothering than our mothers could give us—more fathering than our fathers had to offer—more brothering and sistering than we got from our siblings.
>
> Part of our task in growing up thus becomes finding our own sources of parenting—to add to what our mothers and fathers were not able to give us. We cannot wait for our parents' permission to grow up. We need to decide on our own to find other people to parent us—to find other people to give us what our parents couldn't. To grow up isn't easy, but in

order to do that we must forgive our parents. We must forgive them for our sake, not theirs.[23]

Treatment and wilderness programs and emotional-growth schools all offer other forms of parenting. They don't replace parents; they simply aid in specific areas to promote and resume young people's emotional development. Parents need to forgive themselves, too, for their own as well as their child's sake, to find peace again. All parents are vulnerable to the choices their children make, despite their parenting skills. Children are their own beings and make their own choices. After parents own their patterns, and work to respond in intentional and attuned ways, they have to forgive.

What may be harder for some is forgiving your child. Adolescents and young adults on an emotional rampage often leave disarray in their wake. Lying, stealing, arrests, failure at school, and verbal abuse: the wounds from these offenses take time to heal. Parents are often the punching bags for troubled teens, the target for all their turmoil. Yet with time parents realize it isn't personal; they're simply the safest object in the child's life. Parents can forgive and, with time, rebuild trust.

GRATITUDE

Though at the onset it may seem outlandish to consider it, parents and adolescents across the board come away from the treatment process with a feeling of gratitude. They feel they've grasped something they may not have discovered otherwise. I've consistently seen gratitude in adolescents during the wilderness program. They may not have explicitly said, "Thank you, Mom and Dad, for sending me to treatment." Yet they reliably indicate a sense of relief, acknowledge that wilderness helped them, and, yes, express gratitude. It's a gift to have the opportunity to take a leave of absence from your life, reflect on your choices and behaviors, and examine the areas of deficit. Kids should be grateful that their parents sought out the right treatment and best care for them.

Parents can feel grateful, too, not just because their son or daughter is better equipped to proceed with life, but that they as parents also gained new skills, awareness, and perspective that add to their relationship with their child, and to the larger context of their lives. They may have a new ability to communicate, a deeper reservoir of empathy, a fine-tuned awareness of emotions, and an ability to listen—all of which come with a closer and more enduring bond with their child.

Gratitude brings a softness and openness that can replace the tension and grief. Life is precious and so are children; it's wonderful to strengthen this parent–child bond and move forward to weather storms together, to feel the glue that adheres each to the other. This is all parents can work toward—their own discovery process and letting go.

Grace first had to forgive herself for her emotional sabbatical, and how it had affected her and her children. She then had to forgive her kids, which was easy for her. Gratitude took some time, because for many years she'd viewed herself primarily as a victim. She was locked into the paradigm that life was unfair, that she got a raw deal, and that she'd never be happy again. Yet, through her therapy, she saw that the only thing preventing her from happiness was her belief that she was a victim. When she started to let it go and open fully to her kids, she felt overwhelming gratitude. She felt so lucky and proud to be their mother.

WAKING UP TO THE GIFTS

Parents have a choice. They can learn and grow, see their child as a role model, and read their child's message. Or they can reinforce their negative habits and strengthen damaging patterns, escalating parental anxiety and panic, and entrenching self-protection against the onslaught of life. Mark Epstein describes these struggles:

Compounding the problem is the inevitable estrangement of adolescence, when the first stirrings of grown-up anger make themselves known. Many parents never recover from these upheavals. Their emotional connections with their offspring are so tenuous that when the first expressions of disdain are hurled at them, they retreat forever. Hurt by their children's anger, they feel ignored, unappreciated, wishing for a miracle to restore their importance on their children's lives.[24]

When parents let go of bitterness and resentment that their life was not supposed to be this way, they can wake up to what they have. Gifts surround us: physical health, a home, jobs, children, animals, a sunny day, a favorite meal. Almost everything is uncertain in life; impermanence and change is the nature of all things. However, when parents make a point to appreciate what they have every day, joy can return. Parents can notice the beauty of each day, while still knowing their child is struggling. They can approach their child in treatment with a faith in our own goodness as human beings, rather than fear in the unknown. This opening up to uncertainty is perhaps the best modeling parents can do.

I've come to know many young people at a crossroad in their lives and witnessed the healing process. I've seen how the emotional sensitivity that had seemed like a limitation that made them vulnerable to life's pressures was actually an asset. The sensitivity that led to struggles, and prompted mom and dad to become over-involved, was the same that showed a young person of deep feeling, someone without filters. You might call many of these kids "thin-skinned," yet this ability to feel openly is actually a strength that can steer individuals toward meaningful pursuits.

Through the treatment process, many adolescents and young adults come to feel more at home with their emotions and thoughts. Through the encouragement and validation of feelings, the development of internal resources to manage emotions, and the skills to communicate them, many young people in treatment have honed their own internal mastery, which enables them to access their emotions without spinning into destructive habits or shutting down and withdrawing. This ability to stay with feelings rather than use behaviors to act them out is a way to channel their own natural sensitivity positively. This is a strength. The ability to feel deeply, to access your own vulnerability, are assets in developing close relationships, forming a future family, and perhaps moving into a career to help others. In getting in touch with their own vulnerability, parents too can open up to new possibilities.

THE PARALLEL PROCESS

THIS BOOK IS the result of my being privy for many years to the transformative nature of wilderness therapy in the lives of young people. It felt imperative to share this essential wisdom with the population who needed it most: moms and dads. Not only are the lessons of wilderness interventions beneficial to kids, but as I hope I've shown, the same tenets can be applied in the home and be accessible to all parents. Whatever type of treatment their child is in, parents need these lessons and skills to immerse themselves in a parallel process as a way to catapult themselves back into their child's life, where they're relating on new ground, in a refreshing new way. There is a way to rebuild a bridge between you and your child, to elicit your own courage and compassion.

The fundamental reason wilderness is so effective is that it removes the protective cushion of parents and obliges young people to look at the essence of who they really are. The rawness and nakedness of living outside further removes all escape methods that once kept young people in denial. What's eventually and painstakingly uncovered are underlying emotions, thoughts, and beliefs. Even extremely guarded adolescents who've experienced trauma at a young age and have never let another into their innermost selves, exhibit some degree of softening. Waking with the sun, listening to the birds, talking around a fire at night, living as a group in the middle of nowhere, erodes the thickest walls. Kids begin to relate to each other from a place of authenticity as they shed personas, false identities, and protective armor.

It's as though the harsh elements themselves—the cold nights, strong winds, snowstorms, hail, grueling hikes, raw hands, weeks without showers, and sunburned faces—pulverize the tough shells of young people to reveal the tenderness within. When kids access their own internal world and begin to externalize it, they feel relief. More importantly, they learn to sit with their troubled thoughts, feelings, and beliefs. There's nowhere to run. Sure they still act out and shut down, yet typically that's because they're experiencing their emotions in a more vulnerable way. With time, the defenses subside. Without putting so much energy into erecting walls, kids feel more vigor for life. Through peering into their shadow, with time they begin to smile again. The wilderness experiences provide the freedom to see life as a fresh new canvas. It's commonly referred to as a "wilderness high." Yet how the young people bring their openness, vulnerability, and fearlessness into their life outside of wilderness, their family, and the larger world is the ongoing work that the child and parent must commit to together. When parents engage in a parallel process, join with their child, reinforce the new skills, and employ the same language, they take a step closer to safeguarding this emotional work and build a bridge to their child.

HOW TO ENGAGE IN A PARALLEL PROCESS

I'll admit this process is much harder for parents. Looking within is more onerous and fraught with setbacks for parents. After all, we may be used to anxiously watching from the sidelines, not joining our children in the grueling work of self-examination. Simply seeing that we can contribute, refine our own skills, and get into the game takes a breakthrough in itself. It requires courage, because we don't know what's going to happen; we could fall on our face and fail miserably. Yet, I also want to remind parents that staying on the sidelines can fill us with uncertainty and feelings of powerlessness.

One reason it's harder is that we're older and more set in our ways. Neuroscience reveals that the more pathways in the brain are reinforced and strengthened through set patterns, the harder it is to change.[25] But how do parents buck their own neurology? The same way kids do: through becoming self-aware, refraining, staying put, and trying anything new. Difficult though it is, we're capable of establishing new pathways in the brain, simply by engaging in new behaviors and practicing them—over and over. Many parents say to me, "I'm so fearful my child will never change; he's been taking shortcuts all his life." Yet at the tender age of fifteen, sixteen, seventeen, even twenty-two, kids have much more buoyant and malleable brain tissue. With intentional behavior change and the right reinforcement, kids and adults alike can change.[26]

Neuropsychiatrist Daniel Siegel employs a metaphor of neural pathways as established footpaths through heavy snow.[27] He argues that we're very likely when crossing a field of snow to simply stay on the path that's already been carved out. Yet this is how we reinforce behavioral patterns. Breaking a pattern or an established neural pathway is like tramping through the deep snow, post-holing with each step. It takes foresight, awareness, intentionality, not to mention hard work; but it's possible. Although this path requires perseverance to walk on, it can also lead somewhere new.

The heart of changing our own brain chemistry and our interactions with others is learning how to *stay*: with discomfort, uncertainty, panic—even terror. This is how parents exercise new areas of their brain. We can go for a walk, take deep breaths, and engage in a new hobby—anything to refrain from an unproductive pattern—in attempting to stay open. Kids in the wilderness are removed from their familiar, comfortable environment and "environmental triggers": their bed, cell phone, alley behind the gas station, negative peer, and so on. Parents aren't as lucky. The arena may be different with their child out of harm's way, yet the same unresolved issues are present. This is the exact place where parents need to remain with their feelings, and stay awake and aware.

Let's sum up the three reasons why the process is harder for parents:

1) **Lack of self-awareness**: Parents may not know they're contributing to the problem.
2) **More set stress-responses**: Parents have been strengthening habitual patterns much longer than their child.
3) **Environmental reinforcements**: Parents remain in their comfort zone with access to the same distracters that put them emotionally to sleep.

Despite these obstacles, parents are highly capable of this work. As I mentioned in the previous chapter, people don't change unless their comfort zone becomes uncomfortable. Programs and schools create discomfort for kids who are stagnant and resistant; having a child placed in a therapeutic program can in itself create the degree of chaos needed to disrupt parents' set ways. They may earnestly engage in their own parallel process by utilizing this crisis to begin to address these barriers.

SELF-AWARENESS

As we've seen, this all-encompassing word is the root of the whole process. Self-awareness means becoming aware of behavioral patterns, underlying emotional states, and the ability to be with feelings. The place to start is to identify whether you shut down or lash out during emotional moments. Do you worry, seek control, rescue, withdraw, escalate, distract yourself, avoid a scene, lecture, become stoic, or retreat to an addiction? It cannot be overstated how important it is to engage in some form of self-awareness.

Individual or parent therapy is a critical place to start. Many parents think they're getting enough support from their child's therapist or their child's program. Yet this is another example of blurring boundaries. It's confusing if a parent becomes strongly attached to her daughter's therapist: Is the therapist there for the teen (her client) or her client's mother? When a parent relies heavily on her daughter's therapist, this can often interfere with the child's ability to trust and connect with her therapist (perhaps perpetuating the mother–daughter enmeshment). Parents need their own therapists and their own support systems to examine their own patterns.

Throughout, it's vital to maintain a certain playfulness. In fact, making a game of the task might be just what it takes to break through a parent's self-protection. For instance, a father may admit:

> "Okay, I know I rescue my son. I may not always see that I am doing it, but I am aware that this is my contribution, my part of the problem. So I am going to create a scorecard to tally it up and literally record every incident that I rescue my son in one column. In another column, I am going to ask others, my wife, my therapist, and my son to tell me if I am rescuing, of which I may not be aware. In a third column I am going to record all the times I desperately wanted to help, fix, or problem-solve but refrained."

This is a tremendous exercise in increasing one's self-awareness. It requires vulnerability.

Once a parent has a plan to increase awareness of a pattern, the next step is feeling the underlying emotion. I once worked with a mother who got worked up about any slight setback her daughter faced in treatment. Even though she knew relapses were part of the process, and that the intention of programs was to allow kids to struggle, she still automatically wanted to place the blame somewhere. She felt the program was moving her daughter too quickly, or she disliked her therapist's approach.

When, to highlight her behavior, I pointed out the trajectory of her pattern of worrying, reacting, and trying to fix during each transition throughout her daughter's treatment, the mother was able to identify her core emotion: "I feel terrified to know so little," she revealed. When I asked what she felt when her daughter was sent to wilderness, she was equally emphatic: "Pure terror." Through identifying this feeling, this mother can stop acting out in an effort to find control, and instead learn to stay with her own fears.

STRESS RESPONSES

The next question is: How can parents stay with fear rather than activate their stress response? The mother's terror described above always moved her to blame and catastrophize. Truthfully, this is where parents get stuck. They feel so terrible, they don't care what pattern they might be engaging in. Yet we always have a choice whether to trudge through the heavy snow in a new fresh direction, or reinforce our already established, problematic pathways. Can parents stay and be with their own fears? If we want to courageously roll up our sleeves and work side by side with our child, the answer must be "yes."

Parents can use the angst, anguish, and inner torment as an opportunity for personal growth, and work with these emotions the same way kids in the wilderness do: by compassionately being with their feelings. Therapy, emotional growth, and inner work aren't going to eliminate difficult emotions, but these avenues can teach parents to face these emotions and feel more in-control. The more parents are self-aware, the more they feel internal control, and the more choices they have to change ingrained behaviors. We *can* reframe each time we feel stuck, squeezed, or overwhelmed.

We've noted that parents may have more entrenched response systems; but we're also wiser, having lived more years on the planet. We can reflect on challenging moments and phases we've gone through in our lives and evaluate what helped us. A loss, rejection, or failure may have been painful; but they forced us to rely on our internal resiliency. How did we cope? Did we make healthy or unhealthy choices? We can draw on this reservoir of experiences and see the benefits of hardship. Many parents have erected such strong walls as being "the parent," they lack vulnerability and miss many opportunities to relate and share. If a son is dumped by a girlfriend or a daughter is rejected by a peer, parents can engage in authentic dialogue, while still remaining the parent, and talk about our experiences with the same situation.

During wilderness programs, many parents are asked to write their own life stories. What's struck me time and again is how parents highlight the importance of and lessons learned from struggling. I remember one father describing his experience of starting a business. Each day he felt thrown into the fire, overwhelmed with pressures. Yet he was forced to learn on his feet, and remembered this time as a rich and valuable period. A mother wrote about how it took two divorces to see her pattern of negating her own needs to be able to find the mutually satisfying marriage she now has. There's richness in experiencing adversity, and parents can employ these insights to gain perspective on how they're coping with their child's struggles.

ENVIRONMENT

Parents have not lost the familiar ground of their house, their routine, their job, or their social network as kids have. How do parents propel themselves out of their own nest and set ways while remaining in the same environment? This too is possible. In fact, some programs require change at home, while some parents themselves choose to change.

It cannot be overstated how important it is for parents to seek out therapeutic support: weekly therapy sessions, attending a parent group, or going to Al-Anon. This is often the first step in the process of self-reflecting and gaining awareness, while also providing much-needed emotional support for parents. An essential component to wilderness therapy is the group experience where peers give and receive feedback. This honest dialogue is a crucial part of the process of change because it provides emotional support while offering safe feedback. Through engaging in their own therapy, parents are getting this safe feedback. Therapeutic support can also encourage incorporating more self-care—such as physical exercise, a healthier diet, yoga, meditation, journaling, etc.—into our lives.

Another powerful way to change is to give up a habit or addiction, in order to feel solidarity with your child. As we saw in a previous "conversation" between a son and his father, a parent may give up alcohol or coffee, TV, computer games, gambling, even sugar. Giving up even temporarily whatever habit is most problematic allows parents to sense the discomfort of their child by bravely emulating this at home. Parents might not be self-harming as their kids are, but most aren't coping in emotionally healthy ways. Taking away comforts provides an opportunity to intentionally stay with uneasiness, craving, habitual urges, and angst, and is a giant step toward empathy.

Some parents have even taken to emulating the physical discomforts of wilderness. One father slept on the floor in a sleeping bag during his son's entire wilderness stay. It allowed him to feel a connection to him while he was unable to call or talk to him. Some siblings erect tents outside in an attempt to attune to the missed brother or sister. Going on hikes, noticing nature, watching the stars, becoming more aware of the moon's phases—these too are avenues to your child's experience, and a few of the multiple ways to elicit new feelings and emotions in the familiar setting of the home.

To conclude: Parents don't need to stay on the sidelines, filled with anxiety and uncertainty, acting out habitual patterns and feeling powerless. When parents dirty themselves up, get on their child's level, and stay with the grief, edginess, and panic, they'll see how brave their children are. When parents compassionately remain with their child, without rescuing or fixing, they're on their way to forging a stronger, more intimate, and more empathic bond.

EXPERIMENTING

I've already mentioned the element of playfulness. But we must also experiment. For example, a mother could try for a day or a week only reflecting and mirroring back her child's thoughts and feelings. Parents don't have to do it perfectly; by just responding in a new way, changing the tone, it's possible to create new outcomes. Trial and error is a process of learning.

For example, one boy with explosive anger kept escalating in an attempt to get his mother to manage him. Not knowing what to do, she either walked away to her room for self-preservation or tried to give him what he wanted, with little success. Interacting with her son reliably triggered her own anger; yet trying to escape to her room seemed only to fuel his rage, because he read her behavior as rejection. When this mother attempted emotional attunement and reflective listening (while still holding boundaries) she noticed a new outcome.

"I see you're very angry," she said. "I really want to understand what you're feeling—what your underlying emotion is. Your feelings matter to me. However, I can't listen when you behave this way. I'm ready to listen and understand when you're calmer." She'd never done this before; she was always focused on his behavior and how out of control it was. When she drew attention to her son's internal process and validated him, he felt some relief.

Though she was still unsure, this mother experimented with a new response and was able to see progress. Reflective listening didn't solve her son's anger, but she noticed that he felt heard and it stalled and even de-escalated his rage. Success was variable, yet with time she saw that her old responses were unproductive and, with validation, reflective listening, and emotional attunement, she slowly steered their interactions toward real dialogue.

Whether it's through holding a boundary, validating feelings, empathic listening, "I feel" statements, or identifying your own pattern—experimenting is the only way to make these techniques your own. The fact you're even attempting new responses is a huge step in the right direction. It removes the stress of perfection and disentangling from set responses and established patterns in your relationship with your child. With experimenting, you can be like an attentive researcher, weighing the different outcomes.

YOUR CHOICE

At the end of the day, parents have a choice to be part of the solution and make use of this life experience. Will they contribute to their child's emotional health or not? Many give an unequivocal "yes." Yet few genuinely trudge down this path. It's risky: you have to be vulnerable, shed your self-protection and set beliefs, and jump wholeheartedly into the experience. To engage in a parallel process, parents have to be willing to grow alongside their children. Together, you can face your deepest fears and most ingrained destructive habits together. It's tough, but the Parallel Process enables parents to rediscover the joy and happiness of a healthy relationship with their children.

Good luck with your journey!

appendix

THE BEHAVIOR CONTRACT

I. CONFLICT AGREEMENTS

We understand that all healthy families have conflict. When a conflict arises I (each member of the family) will manage my emotional responses with the following action plan:

Family member 1:

_____

_____

_____

[Example: I will communicate in "I feel" statements. If I am unable to, I will take a time-out for myself and go for a walk or listen to music—depending on the time of day. I will also ask other members of the family to help remind me of this goal if I fall into other behaviors.]

Family member 2:

_____

_____

_____

Family member 3:

_____

_____

_____

Family member 4:

_____

_____

_____

Positive consequences for following through:
- I am reinforcing the skills I learned in treatment.
- I am accountable for my own behavior.
- I am building my communication skills and ability to emotionally regulate.
- I am building trust with my parents and family.

Negative consequences for not following through:
- I am reinforcing negative patterns such as lashing out or shutting down.
- I am not taking accountability for my actions.
- I am not building my communication skills or ability to self-regulate.
- I am losing trust with my parents and family.

II. BEHAVIORAL AGREEMENTS

We will have a weekly family meeting for roughly 30 minutes on _____. During this time we will establish each member's contribution to the family household, family meals, curfews, and any other expectations of the home (computer use, homework time, cell phone minutes, etc.)

Family household contribution:

Family member 1: _____

_____

_____

[*Example: My contribution this week is to cook dinner on Wednesday, clean my room on Friday, and mow the lawn on Saturday.*]

Family member 2: _____

_____

_____

Family member 3: _____

_____

_____

Family member 4: _____

_____

_____

Expectations:
- I will attend _____ (amount) of family dinners each week.
- I will be home at _____ (time) for my curfew.
- I will allocate _____ (amount of time) on my homework each night after dinner.
- I will be on the computer/cell phone/ other technology _____ (amount of time) each night after homework.
- I will commit to one extracurricular activity (sport, club, drama, arts, job outside home, etc.) each semester and maintain full attendance.

Positive consequences for following through:
- If I attend family meetings and family dinners I am building connection and trust with my parents and family members.
- If I honor curfew all week, I will be allowed to stay out an extra hour on both weekend nights—or perhaps with an overnight (depending on level of trust).
- If I responsibly complete my homework, I am building trust with my parents and investing in my future education.
- If I honor the weekday technology time agreements, I will earn _____(amount) additional hours on the weekend.
- If I responsibly complete my household contributions, I will earn my allowance (or other privilege: example, car use, going to a concert, etc.).
- I am building internal resources such as hard work, goal setting, delayed gratification, problem solving, etc., by participating in extracurricular activities (may earn other privileges such as ability to play video games after soccer).

Negative consequences for not following through:
- If I do not attend a family meeting or family dinner (that was not excused), I will lose trust and reciprocity with my parents and family members.
- If I do not honor curfew, the amount of time I was over will be added to my curfew the following evening. If I am late an hour or more (unexcused) then I will be unable to go out the following night.
- If I do not responsibly complete my homework, then I am losing trust with my parents and will be damaging my grades.
- If I use technology inappropriately, my use will be restricted, or potentially taken away.
- If I do not honor my household contributions, I will not earn my allowance (or other privilege).

- I am avoiding the building of internal resources by not participating fully in my chosen extracurricular activity. (Parents may give another consequence such as taking away a privilege—for example to be able to play video games, I have to be engaged in constructive activities first.)

III. THERAPEUTIC AGREEMENTS

- I agree to continue my emotional growth by attending _____(amount) of therapy sessions each week (individual or family).
- I agree to continue to work on healthy peer relations by attending _____(amount) of group therapy each month.
- I agree to maintain my sobriety by attending AA, NA, or another support group _____(amount) each month.
- I agree to evening check-ins with my parents to share thoughts and feelings about the day, where we can give each other feedback and share "I feel" statements.
- I agree to random drug testing.

Positive consequences for following through:
- I continue to grow in my own self-awareness and internal mastery.
- I continue to build healthy peers.
- I recognize sobriety is an on-going commitment.
- I continue to have an open relationship with my parents.
- I pledge to maintain sobriety.

Negative consequences for not following through:
- I am not investing in my mental health and may struggle more as a consequence.
- I am not investing in healthy peer relations.

- I may be more susceptible to relapsing into my addiction.
- I am closing off a relationship with my parents which may interfere with their ability to trust and support me.
- I am likely to relapse.

IV. OTHER IDEAS FOR BEHAVIORAL EXPECTATIONS: (INDIVIDUALIZED TO EACH CHILD'S AGE, AND TREATMENT ISSUES)

- I agree not to have a boyfriend/girlfriend for first three months upon returning home.
- I agree not to be sexually active.
- I agree not to wear Goth (or other) clothing.
- I agree to refrain from reconnecting with drug peers.
- I agree to maintain a B average.
- I agree to not use computer for the first month—then half an hour a day.
- I agree to clean out or close down social media sites.
- I agree to budget _____(amount) of money for shopping for clothes.
- I agree to _____(amount) hours of volunteering to repair my relationship with my school, community, or other.

V. SIGNATURES

In signing this contract, we commit to being accountable to ourselves and our family and to follow through with the contract.

Family member 1: _____

Family member 2: _____

Family member 3: _____

Family member 4: _____

(Note: Home contracts are employed when a child returns home from a treatment program, or used in concert with a day-treatment program or outpatient therapy. This is just an example and can be adjusted to suit the individuality of each child and his or her behavioral and treatment issues. It is critical to have a combination of emotional, behavioral, and therapeutic agreements. Once these agreements are set and in place, parents can just rely on the agreements and consequences in the contract, by following through. Parents will be one step closer to avoiding conflict in the home.)

Websites

- www.parallel-process.com
- www.al-anon.alateen.org
  Find local support groups for family and friends of problem drinkers. Drinking does not have to be the "problem issue" to attend. They're open to all and helpful to meet others whose families are affected by problem behavior.
- www.nami.org
  Helpful information about mental illness and links to local support groups in your area on the "Find Your Local NAMI" page.
- www.strugglingteens.com
  Find information and resources about programs and schools available for struggling teens.
- www.educationalconsulting.org
  Resources for finding an Educational Consultant who can help you find the right school or program for your child.
- www.childrensdisabilities.info/autism/groups-autism-asperger.html
  Support groups for parents of children with autism, Asperger's Syndrome, and Pervasive Development Disorder (PDD)

Books

Beattie, Melody. *Codependent No More: How to Stop Controlling Others and Start Caring for Yourself* (Center City, Minn.: Hazelden, 1992)

Chödrön, Pema. *Taking the Leap: Freeing Ourselves from Old Habits and Fears* (Boston: Shambhala, 2009)

————. *When Things Fall Apart: Heart Advice for Difficult Times* (Boston: Shambhala, 2000)

Gottman, John. *The Relationship Cure: A 5 Step Guide for Building Better Connections with Family, Friends, and Lovers* (New York: Crown Publishers, 2001)

Levine, Madeline. *The Price of Privilege: How Parental Pressure and Material Advantage Are Creating a Generation of Disconnected and Unhappy Kids* (New York: Harper Collins, 2006)

Piper, Mary. *Reviving Ophelia: Saving the Souls of Adolescent Girls New York* (Berkley Publishing Group, 1994)

Ruiz, D. M. *The Four Agreements: A Toltec Wisdom Book* (San Rafael, Calif.: Amber-Allen Publishing, 1997)

Satir, Virginia. *Peoplemaking* (Souvenir Press, 1990)

Simmons, Rachel. *Odd Girl Out: The Hidden Culture of Aggression in Girls* (San Diego: Harvest, 2002)

Twerski, M.D., Abraham. *Addictive Thinking: Understanding Self-Deception* (Center City, Minn.: Hazelden, 1997)

NOTES

1 Kübler-Ross, Elisabeth. *On Death and Dying* (New York: Macmillan, 1969).

2 Berzoff, Joan. (2007) *Inside Out and Outside In: Psychodynamic Clinical Theory and Practice in Contemporary Multicultural Contexts* (Northvale, N.J.: Jason Aronson, 2nd edition, 2007).

3 Bowlby, John. *A Secure Base: Parent–Child Attachment and Healthy Human Development* (New York: Basic Books, 1990).

4 Hallowell, M.D., Edward M., and John J. Ratey, M.D. *Driven to Distraction: Recognizing and Coping with Attention Deficit Disorder from Childhood Through Adulthood* (New York: Touchstone, 1995).

5 Nichols, Michael P., and Richard C. Schwartz. *Family Therapy: Concepts and Methods* (Boston: Allyn and Bacon, 1998) p. 44.

6 Webster's II New Riverside Dictionary (Boston: Houghton Mifflin Company, 1996) p. 230.

7 Katherine, Anne. *Boundaries: Where You End and I Begin* (New York: Fireside, 1991) p. 62.

8 Beattie, Melody. *Codependent No More: How to Stop Controlling Others and Start Caring for Yourself* (Center City, Minn.: Hazelden, 1992)

9 Love, Patricia. *The Emotional Incest Syndrome: What to Do When a Parent's Love Rules Your Life* (New York: Bantam Books, 1990) p. 29.

10 Levine, Madeline. *The Price of Privilege: How Parental Pressure and Material Advantage Are Creating a Generation of Disconnected and Unhappy Kids* (New York: Harper Collins, 2006) p. 141.

11 Heinlein, Robert. *Notebooks of Lazarus Long* (Baen Books, 2004).

12 Levine, Madeline. *op. cit.*, p. 156.

13 Erikson, Erik. (1950) *Childhood and Society* (New York: W.W. Norton and Company, 1950).

14 Bowlby, John. *op. cit.*

15 Siegel, M.D., Daniel, and Mary Hartzell. *Parenting from the Inside Out* (New York: Penguin, 2004) p. 104.

16 Kohn, Alfie. *Unconditional Parenting: Moving from Rewards and Punishments to Love and Reason* (New York: Atria, 2005), p. 179.

17 *Ibid.*, p. 165.

18 Siegel and Hartzell. *op. cit.*, p. 92.

19 *Ibid.*, p. 69.

20 *Ibid.*, p. 85.

21 Gottman, John. *The Relationship Cure: A 5 Step Guide to Strengthening Your Marriage, Family, and Friendships* (New York: Crown, 2001).

22 Minuchin, Salvador. *Family Kaleidoscope* (Cambridge, Mass.: Harvard University Press, 1986).

23 Close, Henry T. "On Parenting," *Voices* 3, Spring, 1968, p. 94. Quoted, with slight changes, in Chapter 3, "No I Won't Grow Up," in *Children of a Certain Age: Adults and Their Unchanging Parents* by Vivian E. Greenberg (Lanham, Md.: Lexington Books, 1999), p. 51.

24 Epstein, M.D., Mark. "Why We Hate Our Parents." *Yoga Journal,* September 12, 2006. <www.yogajournal.com/lifestyle/440> (Accessed August 10, 2010).

25 Siegel, Daniel. "The Clinical Implications of Interpersonal Neuro-biology." See <www.psychotherapynetworker.org/component/con-tent/article/582-compelling-categories?start=3> (Accessed August 10, 2010).

26 The term neuroplasticity means that the brain has the ability to be remolded over time.

27 Siegel, Daniel. "Clinical Implications," *op. cit.*